What Works in Distance Learning: Sample Lessons Based on Guidelines

What Works in Distance Learning: Sample Lessons Based on Guidelines

edited by

Harold F. O'Neil
University of Southern California/CRESST

Information Age Publishing, Inc.
Charlotte, North Carolina • www.infoagepub.com

ISBN 13: 978-1-59311-884-6 (pbk.)

Printed in the United States of America

WHAT WORKS IN DISTANCE LEARNING:
SAMPLE LESSONS BASED ON GUIDELINES

Harold F. O'Neil

University of Southern California/CRESST

Center for the Study of Evaluation
National Center for Research on Evaluation,
Standards, and Student Testing
Graduate School of Education & Information Studies
University of California, Los Angeles
Los Angeles, CA 90095-1522
(310) 206-1532

The work reported herein was supported in part by the Office of Naval Research, under Award No. N00014-04-1-0209, Award No. N00014-02-1-0179, and Award No. N00014-06-1-0711, and in part under the Educational Research and Development Centers Program, PR/Award Number Award Number R305A050004, as administered by the Institute of Education Sciences, U.S. Department of Education. The opinions, findings, and conclusions or recommendations expressed in this material are those of the author(s) and do not reflect the views of the Office of Naval Research, or the positions or policies of the National Center for Education Research, the Institute of Education Sciences, or the U.S. Department of Education. We thank Ms. Katharine Fry for her excellent assistance in preparing the manuscript and Dr. Wallace Wulfeck of the Office of Naval Research for suggesting the use of lessons to support the guidelines.

3

CONTENTS

CHAPTER 1

BACKGROUND AND PURPOSE

Harold F. O'Neil
University of Southern California

The purpose of this book is to document sample lessons based on our *What Works in Distance Learning: Guidelines* (O'Neil, 2005). The intent is to provide an instantiation of our various distance learning guidelines. An overarching goal of our research was to create a robust and clear set of design guidelines and example lessons to support the next generation of distance learning systems.

Each lesson in this book constitutes a case (Mayer, 2005) or partially worked example (Kalyuga, Chandler, Touvinen, & Sweller, 2001). A case is a description of a realistic problem scenario that is relevant to a particular profession or field of study (e.g., a case may be a distance learning lesson showing various instructors trying to design a lesson on a particular topic). A common topic could be, for example, how car brakes work, a surgery procedure, or electronics troubleshooting procedures (Mayer, 2003, 2005). In this book, the case format was useful for the guidelines developed for multimedia strategies, instructional strategies, and assessment strategies. A different format was used for the learning strategies, self-regulation strategies, and management strategies guidelines.

The basic methodology in developing the guidelines for distance learning consisted of a research synthesis, conducted by experts, using analytical methods, on what is known about what works in distance learning. Research in the literature was reviewed for design flaws, and only studies with robust designs were included. Also, we included only those entries for which research evidence and expert opinion were stable and consistent. Furthermore, we decided that this information would be provided to researchers, instructors, program managers, and instructional or assessment designers in a "What Works" format, that is, *What Works in Distance Learning*. We adopted many of the conventions of *What Works: Research About Teaching and Learning* (U.S. Department of Education, 1986, 1987). Our goal for non-researchers was to translate the research findings into clear and comprehensible statements that we think can help users to guide their practice. For both researchers and non-researchers, the references cited for each finding provide an avenue to seek additional information. The guidelines are documented in O'Neil (2005).

Our format conventions for the guidelines were documented in O'Neil (2005) and are quoted here. The conventions were modified from the format conventions of *What Works: Summary of Research Findings With Implementations for Navy Instruction and Learning*

(Montague, 1988). The following format conventions are quoted from that document. The report will "be organized into sections presenting the research synopses. Each gives a short statement presenting the research findings of practical value for the user group. A comment section explains more about the findings and how one might implement conditions that should lead to similar results. References are included for readers who might be interested in the evidence supporting the finding or, in some cases, describing detailed procedures for implementation" (Montague, 1988, p. 2). These format constraints are the same as those in *What Works: Research About Teaching and Learning* (U.S. Department of Education, 1987). Our modifications for the guidelines format consisted of adding (a) a brief section specifying whether a guideline was based on research or expert opinion, (b) a brief rating of the degree of our confidence in the guideline (high, medium, or low), (c) a glossary of terms used, and (d) an indication of the role(s) of the primary users to whom the guideline is addressed,

The sample lessons provided in this book are meant to support the program manager or instructional designer in the use of the guidelines. The method for designing the lessons consists of the following: (a) First, we adopted a content area in which to implement the guidelines (i.e., content dealing with disc brakes; see chapter 2). (b) We began the set of lessons by applying the multimedia guidelines developed by Richard Mayer (chapter 2). Then the instructional strategies guidelines developed by Richard Clark were embedded in the "Mayer" lesson (chapter 3). Finally, the assessment guidelines of Zenaida Aguirre-Muñoz, Jia Wang, and Eva Baker were applied to the Mayer/Clark lesson (chapter 4). (c) The learning strategies and self-regulation strategies guidelines were then instantiated from a trainee perspective in the Mayer/Clark/Aguirre-Muñoz et al. lesson by Myron Dembo and Linda Gubler Junge (chapter 5), and from a self-regulation perspective by Harold O'Neil and San-hui Chuang (chapter 6). (d) Finally, the management strategies guidelines, as they were meant to be applied at the systems level and not at the lesson level, were instantiated with more detail in terms of checklists by Edward Kazlauskas (chapter 7).

The remaining chapters in this book provide the "lessons" for each of the six guideline areas. Each lesson chapter has a common format: (a) title page, (b) abstract, (c) summary of the specific guidelines in the chapter, and (d) the lesson.

CHAPTER 2

MULTIMEDIA STRATEGIES GUIDELINES' LESSON

Richard E. Mayer
University of California, Santa Barbara

Abstract

In *What Works in Distance Learning: Guidelines* (O'Neil, 2005), Mayer (2005) described 11 research-based principles for the design of multimedia training. The principles were based on cognitive theory and supported by empirical scientific research (Clark & Mayer, 2003; Mayer, 2001, 2002; Sweller, 1999).

After the principles have been applied to the lesson on how brakes work, the final product is this chapter, which consists of a concise narrated animation. Our goal was to create a lesson on how brakes work that would lead to deep understanding. Based on a revision of Bloom's taxonomy of educational objectives (Anderson et al., 2001), some major educational objectives of the lesson are:

> *understand conceptual knowledge*—such as being able to describe what happens when you press on the brake pedal;

> *creating conceptual knowledge*—such as being able to redesign a braking system for a new purpose;

> *evaluating conceptual knowledge*—such as being able to troubleshoot a malfunctioning braking system; and

> *understanding factual knowledge*—such as being able to describe what a piston is in your own words.

Overall, the educational objectives are to help students understand conceptual knowledge (e.g., a cause-and-effect model of a braking system) and factual knowledge (e.g., the characteristics of each component in the model) and to help students create and evaluate conceptual knowledge (e.g., revise and critique a cause-and-effect model of a braking system).

Summary

How can we improve a multimedia lesson on how a car's braking system works? For example, let's begin with a text passage that uses printed words to explain a car's barking system (see Text Presentation). Although the passage contains a lot of useful information, learners do not remember most of the steps in the operation of the brakes even on an immediate test (Mayer, 2001). More importantly, learners generally are not able to use the information to solve problems such as "Suppose you step on the brake pedal in your car but the brakes don't work. What could have gone wrong?" (i.e., a troubleshooting problem) or "What could be done to make brakes more effective, that is, to reduce the distance needed to bring the car to a stop?" (i.e., a redesign question). Are there any relevant design principles that are based on empirical scientific research and grounded in cognitive theory? The principles are summarized below.

Multimedia Principle: People learn better from corresponding words and graphics than from words alone. For example, add frames depicting the operation of the braking system in addition to the printed passage describing the operating of the braking system.

Spatial Contiguity Principle: People learn better when corresponding words and graphics are placed near rather than far from each other on the screen. For example, place the printed words that describe a step in the cause-and-effect chain next to the part of a graphic that depicts the same step.

Modality Principle: People learn better from animation and narration than from animation and on-screen text. For example, present animation depicting the steps in the operation of a car's braking system along with narration describing the steps in the operation of a car's braking system.

Personalization Principle: People learn better from multimedia messages when words are in conversational style rather than formal style. For example, the narration about a car's braking system should use words like "I" and "you" and "your."

Voice Principle: People learn better from narrated animation when the narration has a human voice with a standard accent than a machine voice or an accented voice. For example, the narration about a car's braking system should be spoken by a friendly and clear human voice.

Coherence Principle: People learn better from multimedia messages when extraneous words, pictures, and sounds are excluded rather than included. Do not embellish the brakes presentation by adding background sounds or music or interesting but irrelevant details in the form of words or video clips.

Redundancy Principle: People learn better from animation and narration than from animation, narration, and text. Do not add on-screen text to a narrated animation of how brakes work.

Temporal Contiguity Principle: People learn better when corresponding animation and narration segments are presented simultaneously. For example, when the animation depicts a step in the operation of brakes, there should be concurrent narration describing the same step.

Signaling Principle: People learn better from narrated animations when the narration highlights the key steps and the links between them. For example, use louder speech to emphasize the major steps that are described in the narration of how brakes work and use pointer words such as "first, second, third…" to denote the order of the steps.

Prior Knowledge Principle: Low-knowledge learners benefit more from well-designed multimedia messages than do high-knowledge learners. For example, use these principles mainly for people who do not much know about auto mechanics and household repair.

Pre-Training Principle: People learn better from a multimedia presentation when they already know about the components in the presentation. For example, make sure people know about brake pedals, pistons, brake fluid, smaller pistons, brake shoes, and brake drums.

Text Presentation

Suppose you want to explain how a car's braking system works to someone who does not know much about automobile mechanics. A text presentation is a common format for instructional messages.

This is a screenful of printed text describing how brakes work.

When the driver steps on the car's brake pedal, a piston moves forward inside the master cylinder. The piston forces brake fluid out of the master cylinder and through the tubes to the wheel cylinders. In the wheel cylinders, the increase in fluid pressure makes a smaller set of pistons move. These smaller pistons activate the brake shoes. When the brake shoes press against the drum, both the drum and the wheel stop or slow down.

Problem: Novices have difficulty in learning from text alone.

Multimedia Principle

Guideline: People learn better from corresponding words and graphics than from words alone.

A possible solution to the text-only problem is to add graphics.

Two frames have been added to the text—one showing the braking system before the driver steps on the brake pedal and one showing the braking system after the driver steps on the brake pedal. As you can see, the words are near the graphics.

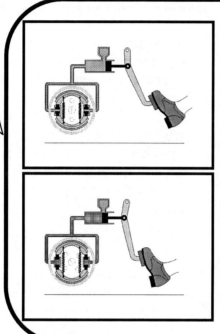

When the driver steps on the car's brake pedal, a piston moves forward inside the master cylinder. The piston forces brake fluid out of the master cylinder and through the tubes to the wheel cylinders. In the wheel cylinders, the increase in fluid pressure makes a smaller set of pistons move. These smaller pistons activate the brake shoes. When the brake shoes press against the drum, both the drum and the wheel stop or slow down.

Solution: In this annotated illustration, the learner is encouraged to make connections between corresponding words and graphics, which results in better learning.

Problem: Can we give the learner more options in receiving the text and graphics?

Spatial Contiguity Principle

Guideline: People learn better when corresponding words and graphics are placed near rather than far from each other on the screen.

As a possible modification to the annotated illustrations, you might be tempted to separate the text and graphics. Your rationale might be that the learner can concentrate on the text and then concentrate on the graphics, and thus gain two exposures to the material. This strategy, however, violates the spatial contiguity principle.

This is a screenful of printed text describing how brakes work.

When the driver steps on the car's brake pedal, a piston moves forward inside the master cylinder. The piston forces brake fluid out of the master cylinder and through the tubes to the wheel cylinders. In the wheel cylinders, the increase in fluid pressure makes a smaller set of pistons move. These smaller pistons activate the brake shoes. When the brake shoes press against the drum, both the drum and the wheel stop or slow down.

See graphics

When you click on "See graphics" you see these graphics depicting how brakes work.

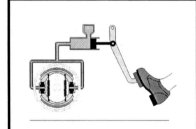

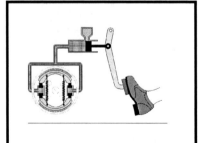

Problem: When graphics are separated from the text, learners have difficulty in making connections between corresponding words and graphics.

Return

**Spatial Contiguity Principle
(continued)**

According to the spatial contiguity principle, corresponding graphics and words should be near each other on the screen, as in this screen.

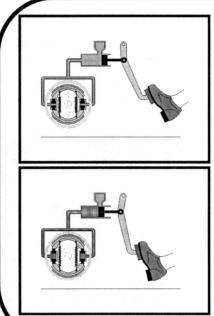

When the driver steps on the car's brake pedal, a piston moves forward inside the master cylinder. The piston forces brake fluid out of the master cylinder and through the tubes to the wheel cylinders. In the wheel cylinders, the increase in fluid pressure makes a smaller set of pistons move. These smaller pistons activate the brake shoes. When the brake shoes press against the drum, both the drum and the wheel stop or slow down.

Solution: In this annotated illustration, the learner is encouraged to make connections between corresponding words and graphics, which results in better learning.

Problem: Can we use animation rather than static illustrations?

Text and Animation Presentation

The brakes graphics have been converted into an animation depicting the operation of the braking system, with corresponding words presented as on-screen text at the bottom of the screen.

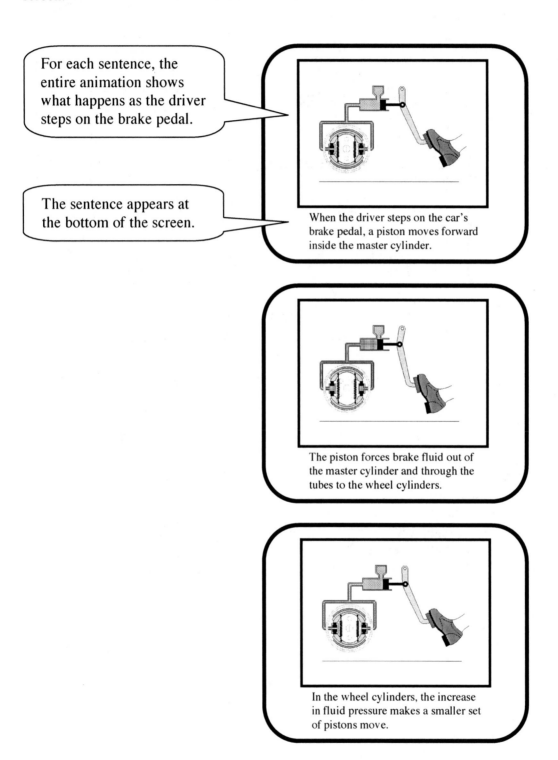

For each sentence, the entire animation shows what happens as the driver steps on the brake pedal.

The sentence appears at the bottom of the screen.

When the driver steps on the car's brake pedal, a piston moves forward inside the master cylinder.

The piston forces brake fluid out of the master cylinder and through the tubes to the wheel cylinders.

In the wheel cylinders, the increase in fluid pressure makes a smaller set of pistons move.

Text and Animation Presentation
(continued)

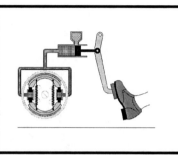

These smaller pistons activate the brake shoes.

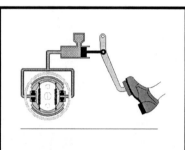

When the brake shoes press against the drum, both the drum and the wheel stop or slow down.

Problem: The learner must try to read the words and view the animation at the same time. This could overload the learner's visual system.

Modality Principle

Guideline: People learn better from animation and narration than from animation and on-screen text.
A solution to the split attention problem is to present spoken words rather than printed words, thus reducing the load on the visual system.

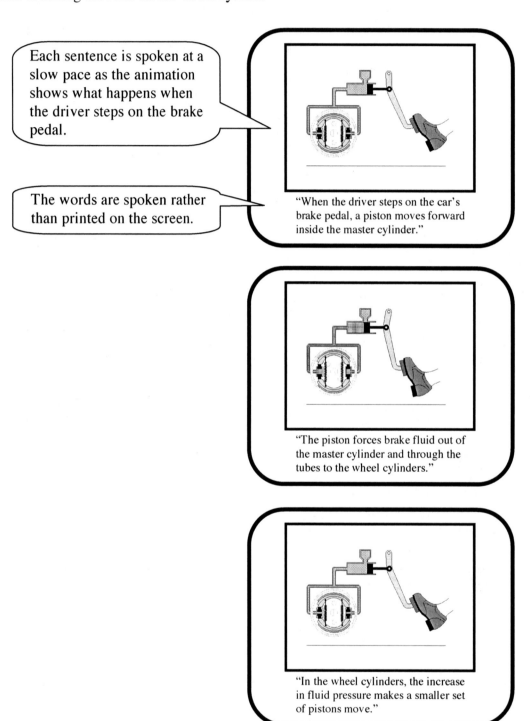

Each sentence is spoken at a slow pace as the animation shows what happens when the driver steps on the brake pedal.

The words are spoken rather than printed on the screen.

"When the driver steps on the car's brake pedal, a piston moves forward inside the master cylinder."

"The piston forces brake fluid out of the master cylinder and through the tubes to the wheel cylinders."

"In the wheel cylinders, the increase in fluid pressure makes a smaller set of pistons move."

Modality Principle
(continued)

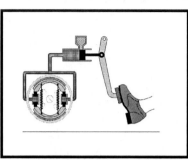

"These smaller pistons activate the brake shoes."

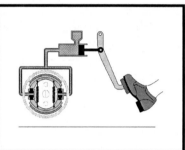

"When the brake shoes press against the drum, both the drum and the wheel stop or slow down."

Solution: The learner can hold corresponding words and images in working memory at the same time.

Problem: How can we help the learner feel like the computer is a social partner?

Personalization Principle

Guideline: People learn better from multimedia messages when words are in conversational style rather than formal style.
A possible improvement is to use conversational style including words such as "I" and "you." The goal is to help learners feel as if they are in a conversation with the computer, so they will try harder to understand.

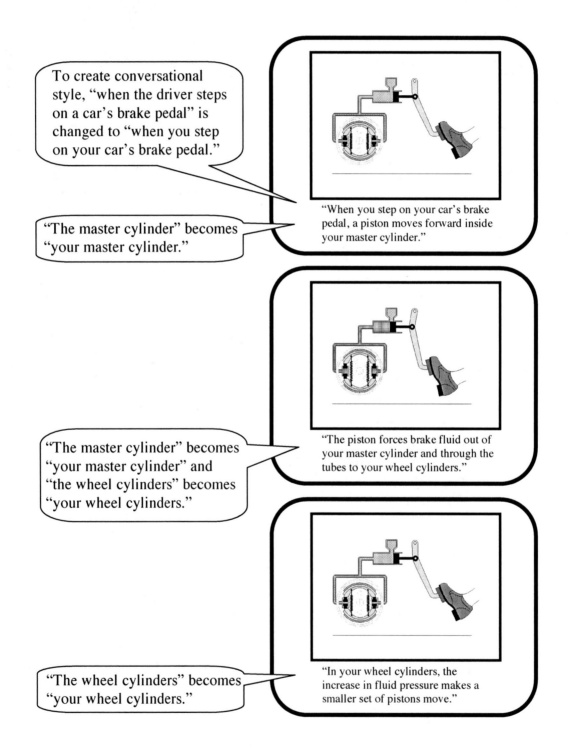

To create conversational style, "when the driver steps on a car's brake pedal" is changed to "when you step on your car's brake pedal."

"The master cylinder" becomes "your master cylinder."

"When you step on your car's brake pedal, a piston moves forward inside your master cylinder."

"The master cylinder" becomes "your master cylinder" and "the wheel cylinders" becomes "your wheel cylinders."

"The piston forces brake fluid out of your master cylinder and through the tubes to your wheel cylinders."

"The wheel cylinders" becomes "your wheel cylinders."

"In your wheel cylinders, the increase in fluid pressure makes a smaller set of pistons move."

**Personalization Principle
(continued)**

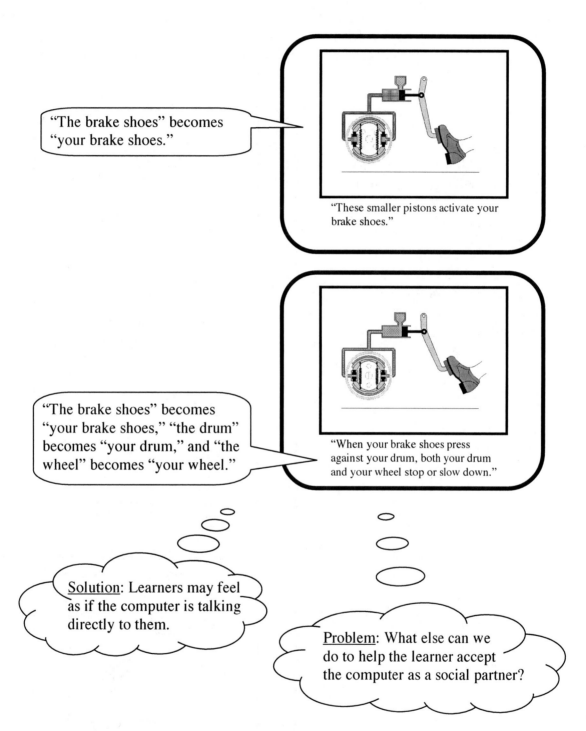

Voice Principle

Guideline: People learn better from narrated animation when the narration has a human voice with a standard accent rather than a machine voice or an accented voice.
Another possible way to create a sense of social partnership is to use a standard accented human voice that the learners interpret as friendly, intelligent, and dynamic. The rationale is that learners may try harder to understand when they accept the speaker as a social partner.

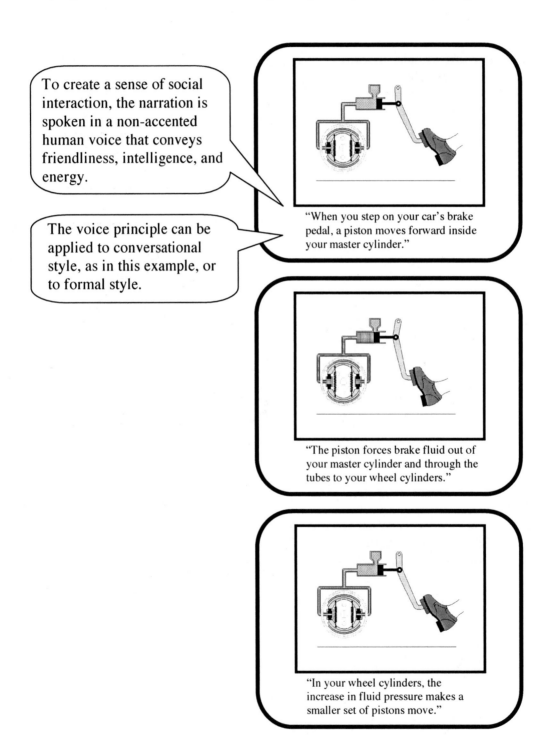

To create a sense of social interaction, the narration is spoken in a non-accented human voice that conveys friendliness, intelligence, and energy.

The voice principle can be applied to conversational style, as in this example, or to formal style.

"When you step on your car's brake pedal, a piston moves forward inside your master cylinder."

"The piston forces brake fluid out of your master cylinder and through the tubes to your wheel cylinders."

"In your wheel cylinders, the increase in fluid pressure makes a smaller set of pistons move."

Voice Principle
(continued)

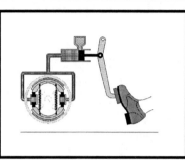

"These smaller pistons activate your brake shoes."

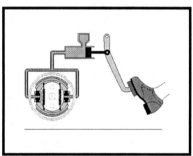

"When your brake shoes press against your drum, both your drum and your wheel stop or slow down."

Solution: Learners may feel as if the computer is talking directly to them.

Problem: Can we spice up the lesson with some interesting additions?

Coherence Principle (#1)

Guideline: People learn better from multimedia messages when extraneous words, pictures, and sounds are excluded rather than included.

It may be tempting to embellish a presentation by adding background sounds or music. However, the added materials can distract the learner and disrupt the learner's building of a causal chain.

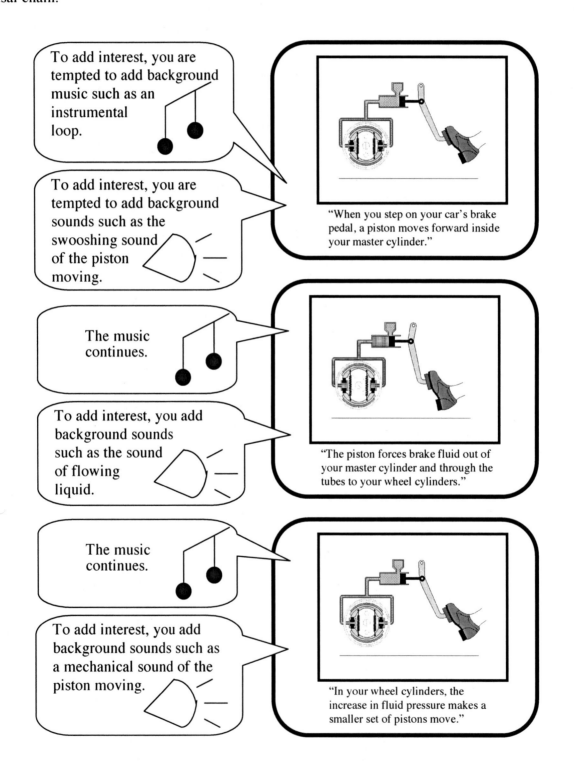

Coherence Principle (#1)
(continued)

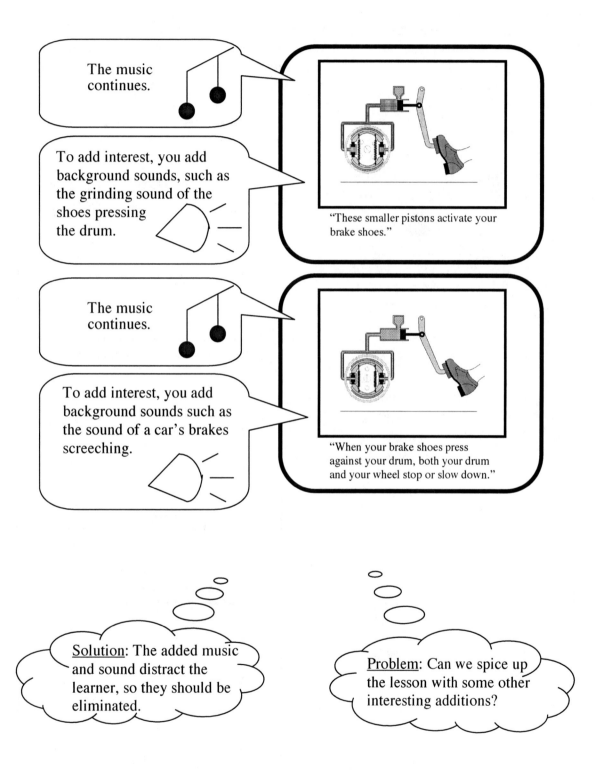

Coherence Principle (#2)

Guideline: People learn better from multimedia messages when extraneous words, pictures, and sounds are excluded rather than included.
Although background music and sounds might violate the coherence principle, you may be tempted to embellish a presentation by adding interesting details in the narration or adding interesting graphics. However, the added materials can distract the learner, disrupt the learner's building of a causal chain, and encourage the learner to mentally relate the material to inappropriate prior knowledge.

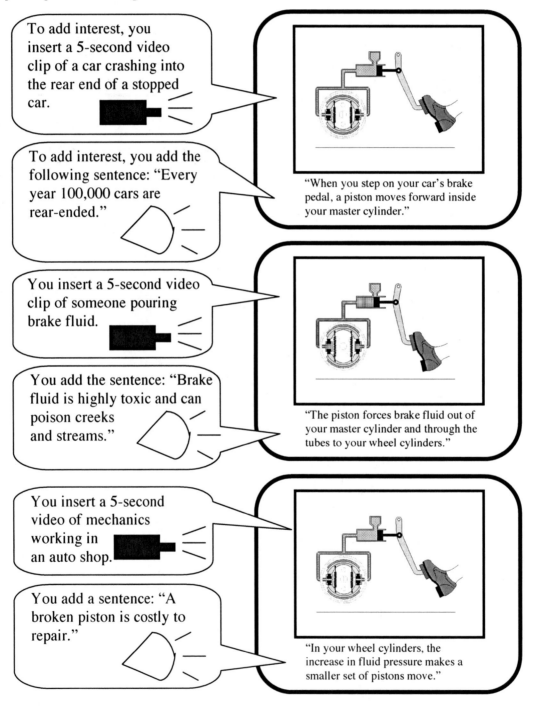

Coherence Principle (#2)
(continued)

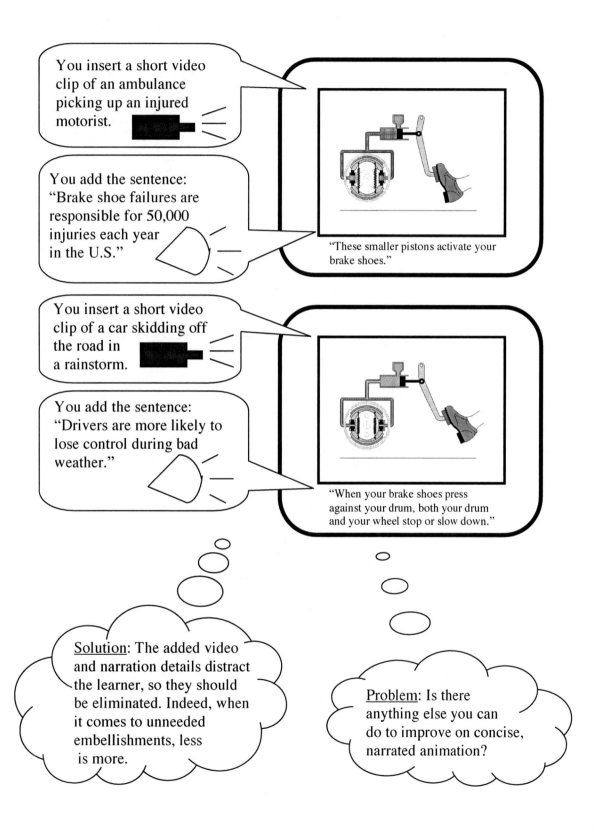

You insert a short video clip of an ambulance picking up an injured motorist.

You add the sentence: "Brake shoe failures are responsible for 50,000 injuries each year in the U.S."

"These smaller pistons activate your brake shoes."

You insert a short video clip of a car skidding off the road in a rainstorm.

You add the sentence: "Drivers are more likely to lose control during bad weather."

"When your brake shoes press against your drum, both your drum and your wheel stop or slow down."

Solution: The added video and narration details distract the learner, so they should be eliminated. Indeed, when it comes to unneeded embellishments, less is more.

Problem: Is there anything else you can do to improve on concise, narrated animation?

Redundancy Principle

People learn better from animation and narration than from animation, narration, and text.
You may be tempted to embellish a narrated animation by adding on-screen text. Your rationale might be that when the learner has access to words in spoken and printed form she can choose the format she prefers. However, the on-screen text can detract from learning because the learner must split her visual attention between the on-screen text and the animation. The on-screen text also can detract from learning because the learner must use limited cognitive processing to reconcile the printed and spoken words.

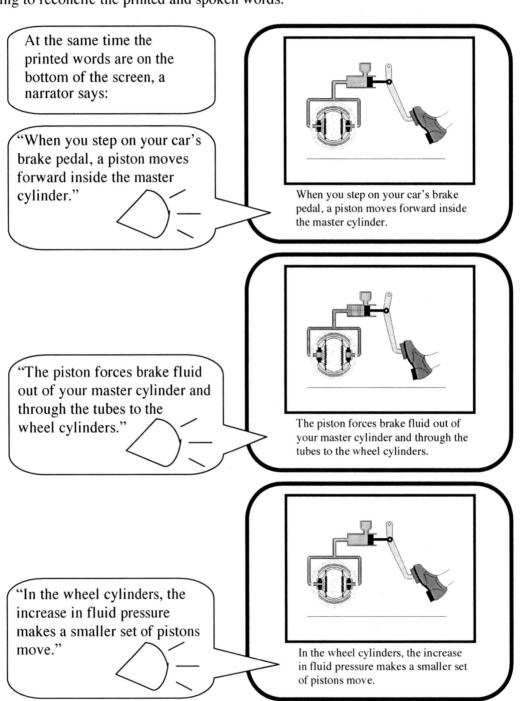

At the same time the printed words are on the bottom of the screen, a narrator says:

"When you step on your car's brake pedal, a piston moves forward inside the master cylinder."

When you step on your car's brake pedal, a piston moves forward inside the master cylinder.

"The piston forces brake fluid out of your master cylinder and through the tubes to the wheel cylinders."

The piston forces brake fluid out of your master cylinder and through the tubes to the wheel cylinders.

"In the wheel cylinders, the increase in fluid pressure makes a smaller set of pistons move."

In the wheel cylinders, the increase in fluid pressure makes a smaller set of pistons move.

Redundancy Principle
(continued)

"These smaller pistons activate the brake shoes."

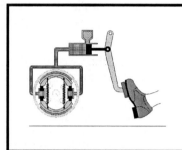

These smaller pistons activate the brake shoes.

"When the brake shoes press against the drum, both the drum and the wheel stop or slow down."

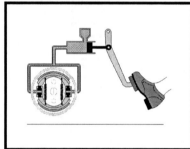

When the brake shoes press against the drum, both the drum and the wheel stop or slow down.

Solution: The added on-screen text draws the learner's visual attention away from the animation and encourages the learner to waste cognitive processing by comparing the spoken and printed text. The solution is to avoid redundant on-screen text.

Problem: Is there anything you can do to improve on a concise, narrated animation?

Temporal Contiguity Principle

Guideline: People learn better when corresponding animation and narration segments are presented simultaneously.

You may be tempted to embellish the multimedia presentation by allowing the learner to view the animation separately from hearing the narration. For example, when the learner clicks on a movie icon, the animation is presented on the screen; when the learner clicks on the speaker icon, the narration is presented through the head phones. Your rationale might be that the learner will have two presentations of the same explanation and can focus on each one. However, presenting the corresponding words and graphics at different times makes it hard for the learner to make connections between corresponding words and pictures—a major step in understanding. Thus, your embellishment violates the temporal contiguity principle.

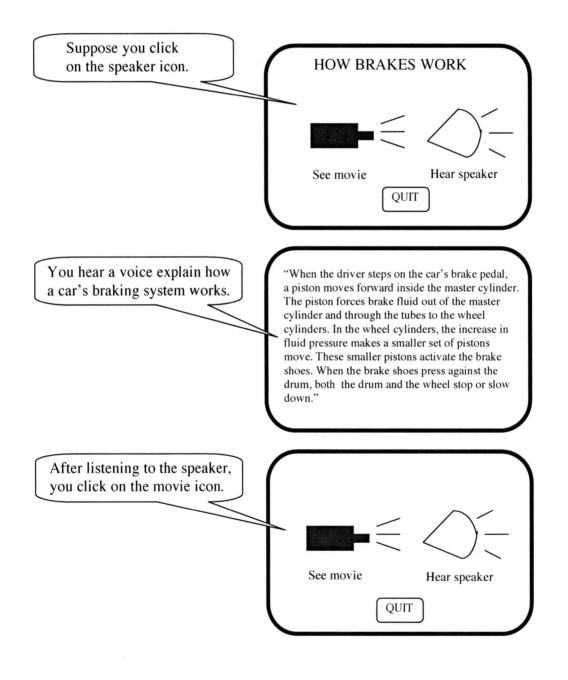

Temporal Contiguity Principle
(continued)

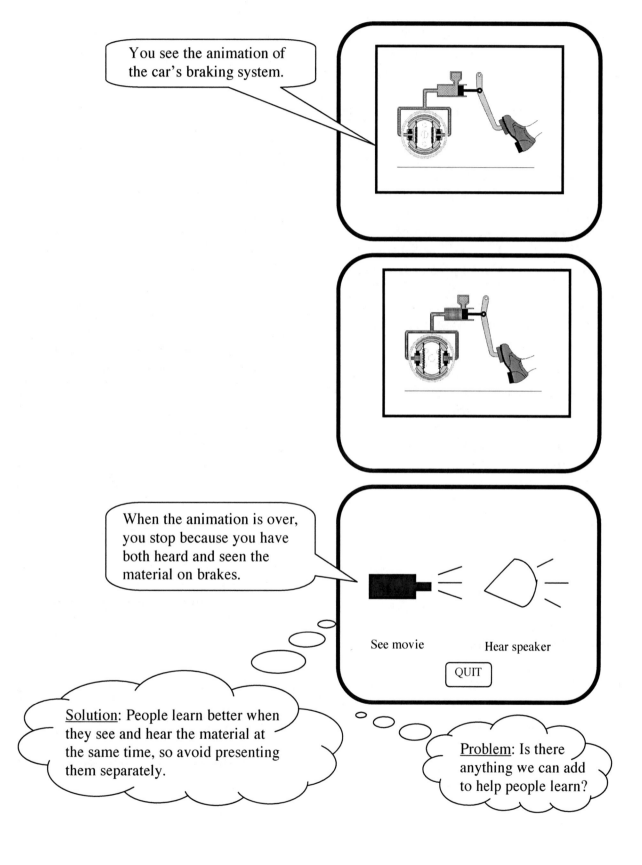

Signaling Principle

Guideline: People learn better from narrated animations when the narration highlights the key steps and the links between them.

So far, all of the ways of embellishing narrated animations have hurt learning. Signals are words that are added to the narration that emphasize important material and help outline the structure of the material. Signals, however, do not provide any new content. Signals are intended to help learning by providing cues to the learner about how to process the presented words and pictures; that is, they guide the learner in selecting relevant information and organizing it.

The first aspect of signaling is to provide an **outline sentence**. Thus, the narrator inserts this sentence outlining the steps in the braking sequence: "There are eight steps in braking: (1) driver steps on brake pedal, (2) piston moves forward, (3) forces brake fluid out, (4) increase in pressure, (5) smaller pistons move, (6) activate brake shoes, (7) press against drum, (8) drum stops."

"First, when the driver **steps** on the car's brake pedal, a piston **moves forward** inside the master cylinder."

The second aspect of signaling is to add **highlighting** such as emphasizing the key actions through louder and deeper speech. The highlighted words are indicated in bold in each of the frames shown.

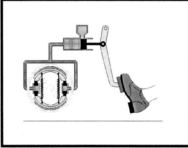

"Next, the piston **forces** brake fluid out of the master cylinder and through the tubes to the wheel cylinders."

The third aspect of signaling is to add **pointer words**, such as "first, second, third…" or "because of this" or "as a result." The word "First" was added to the first sentence, "Next" was added to the second sentence (in this frame), "Then" was added to the third sentence, "As a result" is added to the fourth sentence, and "Finally" is added to the last sentence.

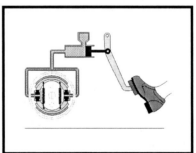

"Then, in the wheel cylinders, the **increase** in fluid pressure makes a smaller set of pistons **move.**"

Signaling Principle
(continued)

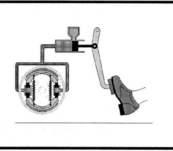

"As a result, these smaller pistons **activate** the brake shoes."

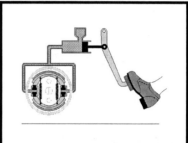

"Finally, when the brake shoes **press against** the drum, both the drum and the wheel **stop** or **slow down**."

Solution: Signals such as these can improve learning by guiding the learner's cognitive processing during learning.

Problem: Do these principles apply equally well to all learners, such as learners with low and high prior knowledge of the topic?

Prior Knowledge Principle

Guideline: Low-knowledge learners benefit more from well-designed multimedia messages than do high-knowledge learners.
For example, consider the multimedia principle which states people learn better from corresponding words and graphics than from graphics alone. This principle works best for learners who lack knowledge about the topic, but not for learners who possess a lot of knowledge about the topic.

To assess prior knowledge related to car braking systems, we can ask learners to indicate their past behaviors and events, such as in a checklist. For example, the learner receives one point for each checked item.

Please put an "x" next to the things you have done:
___ I have obtained a driver's license.
___ I have put air into a car's tire.
___ I have changed a tire on a car.
___ I have changed oil in a car.
___ I have installed spark plugs in a car.
___ I have replaced the brake shoes in a car.

To assess prior knowledge related to car braking systems, we can ask learners to rate their knowledge of car mechanics and repair. For example, the learner receives 1 point for "very little" and 5 points for "a lot" and so on.

Please place a check mark indicating your knowledge of car mechanics and repair:

___ A lot
___
___ Average
___
___ Very little

Some of the high-knowledge learners and some of the low-knowledge learners receive a poorly designed presentation on brakes consisting only of narration (or narration followed by animation). With poorly designed presentations, high-knowledge people learn much better than the low-knowledge people.

"When the driver steps on the car's brake pedal, a piston moves forward inside the master cylinder. The piston forces brake fluid out of the master cylinder and through the tubes to the wheel cylinders. In the wheel cylinders, the increase in fluid pressure makes a smaller set of pistons move. These smaller pistons activate the brake shoes. When the brake shoes press against the drum, both the drum and the wheel stop or slow down."

Prior Knowledge Principle
(continued)

Some of the high-knowledge learners and some of the low-knowledge learners receive a well-designed presentation on brakes consisting of concurrent animation and narration. With well-designed presentations, low-knowledge people learn as well as high-knowledge people.

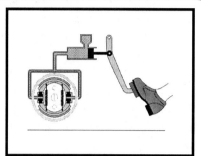

"When the driver steps on the car's brake pedal, a piston moves forward inside the master cylinder."

Solution: The design principles may be more effective for learners who lack prior knowledge. High-knowledge learners may even be distracted by some of the aids intended to promote learning.

Problem: Is there a way to provide appropriate knowledge?

Pre-Training Principle

Guideline: People learn better from a multimedia presentation when they already know about the components in the presentation.

When learners view an animation while listening to a corresponding narration, they are exposed to a lot of information in a short time. For example, in the brakes presentation they must try to understand how each part works—such as the brake pedal, the piston in the master cylinder, the brake fluid, the smaller pistons in the wheel cylinders, the brake shoes, and the drum. In addition, they must try to build a causal chain in which a change in one part causes a change in the next part, and so on—such as stepping on the brake pedal causes a piston to move forward, which causes the brake fluid to compress, which causes smaller pistons to move, and so on. If learners do not know the name, location, and behavior of each part, they must focus their attention on locating the part and may not have attention left over to build a causal chain. This problem can be alleviated by providing pre-training in the name, location, and behavior of each part.

For example, to provide pre-training concerning the name and location of each part, we can show the learner a labeled map. As you can see, this labeled map shows the name and location of six parts of the braking system.

To provide pre-training in the behavior of each part, we can allow the learner to click on each part. Then a message appears describing the actions of the part. For example, when the learner clicks on the piston in the master cylinder, the following text appears on the screen next to the piston: "This is the piston in the master cylinder. It can move either Back or Forward."

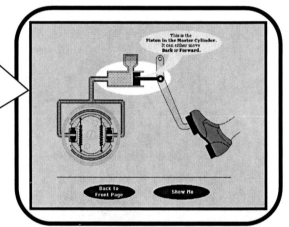

To provide further pre-training about the behavior of each part, the learner can click on the "SHOW ME" button. For example, after selecting the piston in the master cylinder and pressing on the "SHOW ME" button, the learner sees a short animation of the piston moving forward and back while the rest of the braking system is blacked out.

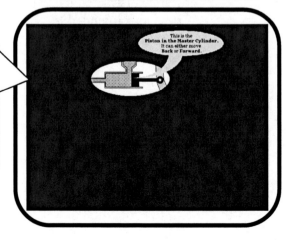

Pre-Training Principle
(continued)

When the animation ends, the screen returns to the labeled map and the learner can click on the next part and so on. After learning about the name, location, and behavior of each part, the learner can click the DONE button to see the narrated animation of the braking system.

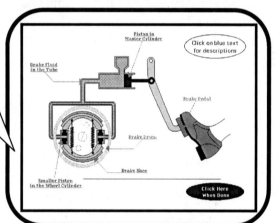

After receiving pre-training about the parts in the braking system, the learner can devote her full attention to building connections from one step to the next in the causal explanation.

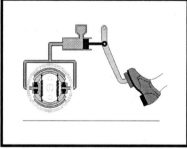

"When the driver steps on the car's brake pedal, a piston moves forward inside the master cylinder."

Solution: Students who lack prior knowledge can understand a concise narrated animation better if they get pre-training about the name, location, and behavior of each part.

An Exemplary Lesson: Concise Narrated Animation

We began with a text explanation of how a car's braking system works and ended up with a concise narrated animation. The only embellishments that improved the concise narrated animation were signals, personalization, voice, and pre-training. This well-designed presentation may be most effective for learners who lack experience and knowledge in the topic.

Before presenting the multimedia lesson, it is worthwhile to consider the characteristics of the learner, such as the learner's prior knowledge. This is part of a questionnaire intended to assess the learner's prior knowledge about brakes. According to the *prior knowledge principle*, we should apply the design principles to low-knowledge learners.

Please place a check mark indicating your knowledge of car mechanics and repair:

____ A lot

____ Average

____ Very little

Before presenting the multimedia lesson to low-knowledge learners, it is worthwhile to provide some pre-training concerning each component in the system. This graphic follows the *pre-training principle* because it shows the name of each part of the system: brake pedal, piston in master cylinder, brake fluid in the tube, smaller piston, brake shoe, and brake drum.

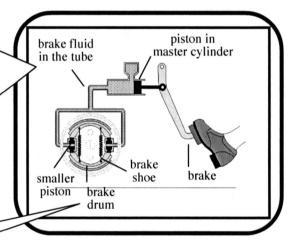

This graphic also follows the *spatial contiguity principle* because the printed words are placed next to the part of the graphic they describe. For example, the words "brake drum" are placed next to the graphic of the brake drum.

An Exemplary Lesson: Concise Narrated Animation
(continued)

This is a screenful of concise narrated animation explaining how brakes work.

It follows the *multimedia principle* because it includes both words (i.e., narration) and graphics (i.e., animation).

It follows the *modality principle* because it presents words as narration rather than as on-screen text. (The quotation marks indicate that the words are spoken.)

It follows the *redundancy principle* because it does not have on-screen text in addition to the narration.

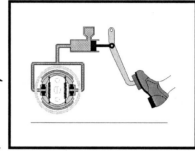

"First, when you **step** on your car's brake pedal, a piston **moves forward** inside your master cylinder."

It follows the *personalization principle* because it uses "you" instead of the "the driver" and "your" instead of "the."

It follows the *voice principle* because the speaker has a human voice with a standard accent.

It follows the *signaling principle* because the speaker emphasizes key words such as "forces."

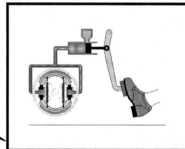

"Next, the piston **forces** brake fluid out of your master cylinder and through the tubes to your wheel cylinders."

It follows the *coherence principle* because it is concise: It has no extraneous sounds or music, no extraneous words, and no extraneous graphics.

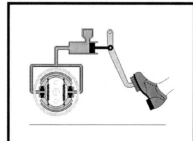

"Then, in your wheel cylinders, the **increase** in fluid pressure makes a smaller set of pistons **move.**"

**An Exemplary Lesson: Concise Narrated Animation
(continued)**

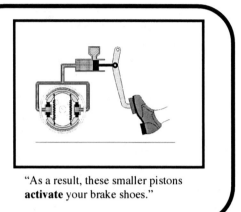

"As a result, these smaller pistons **activate** your brake shoes."

It follows the *temporal contiguity principle* because corresponding animation and narration segments are presented simultaneously. For example, the animation depicts the shoes pressing against the drum at the same time that the narration says "your brake shoes press against the drum."

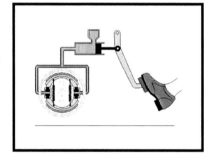

"Finally, when your brake shoes **press against** the drum, both your drum and your wheel **stop** or **slow down**."

If the words are printed as on-screen text (which in some cases would violate the modality principle), then the *spatial contiguity principle* recommends that the printed words should be placed next to the part of the animation they describe. For example, these words should be printed near to the brake shoes.

Solution: The concise narrated animation can help novices learn better than the text presentation we started with.

CHAPTER 3

INSTRUCTIONAL STRATEGIES GUIDELINES' LESSON

Richard E. Clark
University of Southern California

Abstract

In *What Works in Distance Learning: Guidelines* (O'Neil, 2005), Clark (2005) presented nine design principles for instructional strategies. This chapter presents concrete examples of how to apply the nine instructional strategies to a lesson on how a car's barking system works and how to change brake shoes. It builds on the prior chapter by Mayer. The chapter begins with instructions on how to teach four of the most common types of knowledge: concepts (What is this?), processes (How does it work?), causal principles (What is the cause and effect?), and procedures (How do I do this?). After the discussion of principles, the chapter describes how to provide worked examples to illustrate the solving of problems based on principles and how to give feedback when students make mistakes while they are learning. Then the chapter turns to suggested ways to increase learners' motivation to actively engage in learning and to persist despite distractions by suggesting the value of having mastered the knowledge and skills being taught and the utility of avoiding the problems caused by not learning. Learner confidence and mental effort are encouraged by giving learners feedback that reminds them of their success at specific tasks. Mental effort is encouraged by pointing out that their success is due, in part, to thinking carefully about how to solve the problems before they begin.

Summary

How can you improve the instructional design strategies you build into a multimedia lesson? In this section, design strategies will be illustrated in a lesson on how a car's braking system works and how to troubleshoot and fix brake problems.

You decide on instructional strategies after you have decided what you will teach (as a result of needs analysis and task analysis) and in what order you will teach it. This section will help you decide what instructional strategies are best for designing instruction for the four primary types of knowledge (concepts, processes, principles, and procedures). It will also describe ways to give students worked examples to illustrate how to solve problems or how to implement procedures, and how to design feedback that corrects errors without discouraging learners. In addition, motivational strategies are described that will increase learners' active engagement with a lesson, and lead them to persist at learning and problem solving despite distractions and to invest maximum mental effort to achieve learning goals.

This chapter begins with a design for one of the most frequently taught kinds of knowledge—a *concept* (What/where is this thing?). Teaching concepts requires that learners acquire an accurate definition (with key elements in the definition highlighted to draw attention to them) and one or more examples that, if possible, should be familiar in the setting where the knowledge will be applied.

The second instructional strategy is focused on the teaching of *processes* (How does this work?). The best strategy for teaching a process is to describe (for example, in a flowchart) all stages in the process, what happens at each stage, how stages may be linked to each other and what happens at the end of the process. Where possible, it is useful to give a concrete example of the operation of a specific process in a simulation based on the work setting.

Cause and effect *principles* are often taught in problem-solving lessons. These principles are often stated in an "If-Then" format—If (this cause happens), Then (the cause will change an effect to some known value in the future); or If (you want to know the value of some outcome), Then (implement this set of causes and you will achieve the specific value of this outcome in the future). Principles are taught by stating the principle and giving an example of the use of the principle to solve a problem.

Procedures (How do I do this?) are taught by stating all of the steps in the procedure, and then demonstrating the procedure using a model or a simulation. There are usually two types of steps in procedures: actions (What overt physical actions are necessary now?) and decisions (What criteria should I apply to decide between these alternatives at this point?). The *worked example* instructional strategy is designed to help you plan ways to provide a worked example of a way to solve a problem or implement a procedure. When instruction provides clear (to the learner) and complete procedural "how to" examples of the decisions and actions needed to solve problems and perform necessary tasks to be learned, then learning and transfer will be increased.

When students are practicing problem solving based on principles or learning concepts, or processes or procedures, they often make mistakes. To correct mistakes you must plan to give students *feedback*. The feedback instructional strategy describes ways that you can build in effective feedback during multimedia instruction. Recent experiments on feedback suggest that the more it (a) is based on concrete learning goals that are clearly understood by learners, (b) describes the gap between the learning goal and the learner's current performance and suggests how to close that gap, and (c) focuses the student's attention on the learning goal and not on his/her mistake or failure to achieve the goal, the more effective it becomes for learners, learning, and transfer of learning to performance settings.

Since not all learners are equally motivated and since everybody experiences lapses in *motivation* during instruction, the motivation instructional strategies are designed to increase the active engagement and persistence of learners in multimedia instruction. Designers can help students to become *actively engaged* in a course or lesson and to *persist or stay "on track"* when distracted by helping students connect their personal goals and interests to course goals, by clearly communicating the utility of the course goals (and the risk of not achieving them), and by helping students maintain their confidence in achieving the course goals by pointing out past successes with similar goals.

Moreover, the more that learners are convinced that the important elements of a learning task are novel to them, the more mental effort they will invest to succeed. Conversely, the more that students believe that a learning task is familiar, the more overconfident they become, the less mental effort they invest to learn, and the less they are inclined to accept responsibility for failure to learn. Finally, for relevant guidelines, a designer's learning objective and a trainee's learning objective are provided.

Teaching Concepts
(A concept is any term that has a definition and at least one example.)

To teach a concept, list all defining characteristics (key elements) of the concept and provide a concrete example.

DESIGNER'S LEARNING OBJECTIVE: You will learn how to design instruction for teaching concepts by providing the name of the concept and a list of the key elements of each concept, and by giving trainees at least one concrete example of each concept where the key elements are labeled.

TRAINEE'S LEARNING OBJECTIVE: You will learn how to define the concept of "Brake Master Cylinder" by describing its key elements and their function in stopping a vehicle.

CONCEPT—Brake Master Cylinder
Definition: A **metal cylinder**, containing a small, **movable piston** that is **connected to the brake pedal** on one side, and a **metal tube** that extends to the brake cylinder on the other side. The master cylinder is **filled with hydraulic brake fluid**. As you apply pressure on the brake pedal with your foot, it **forces** the small movable piston in the brake master cylinder to push the **hydraulic fluid into the metal tube** on the other side of the cylinder to force the brake linings against your wheel drum to slow down or stop your car. See the **example** below:

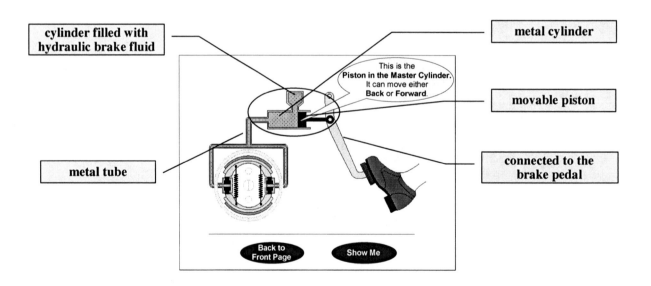

Instructional Design to Teach a Process
(How Something Works)

Integrate pictures (or animation) and verbal (print or narrative) description of each of the stages in the process, in their exact sequence. Describe what happens at each stage.

DESIGNER'S LEARNING OBJECTIVE: You will learn to design instruction to teach a process by describing and explaining the sequence of events that occur in the process to be learned by trainees.

TRAINEE'S LEARNING OBJECTIVE: You will learn to describe how the brakes in a car work by describing each stage in the process that starts when a person steps on the brake pedal and ends when the car slows or stops.

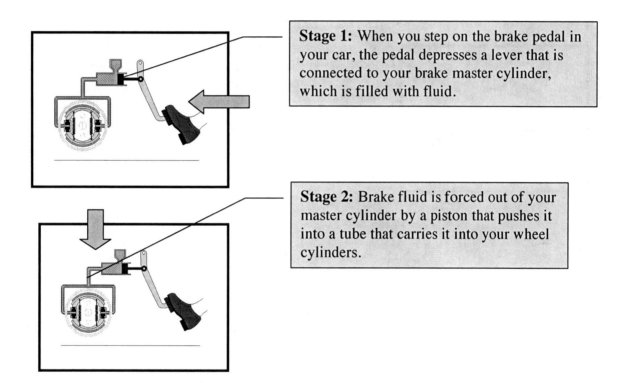

Stage 1: When you step on the brake pedal in your car, the pedal depresses a lever that is connected to your brake master cylinder, which is filled with fluid.

Stage 2: Brake fluid is forced out of your master cylinder by a piston that pushes it into a tube that carries it into your wheel cylinders.

Instructional Design to Teach a Process
(How Something Works)
(continued)

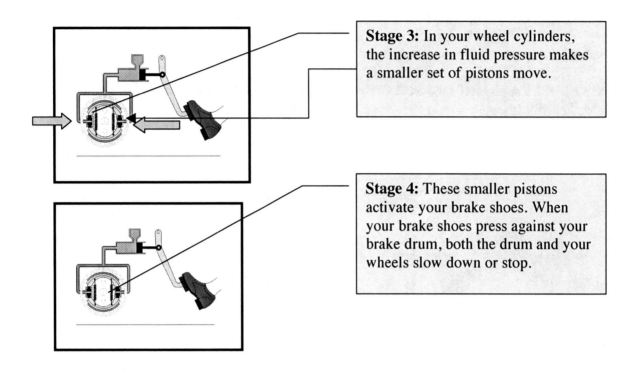

Stage 3: In your wheel cylinders, the increase in fluid pressure makes a smaller set of pistons move.

Stage 4: These smaller pistons activate your brake shoes. When your brake shoes press against your brake drum, both the drum and your wheels slow down or stop.

Instructional Design to Teach a Principle

Below is an example of a principle for determining the "stopping distance" of a braking vehicle and how to compute the distance covered by a vehicle from the moment the brakes are applied until it comes to a stop using the "stopping distance" principle.

DESIGNER'S LEARNING OBJECTIVE: You will learn how to design instruction for teaching a "cause and effect" principle by stating the cause(s) and resulting effect(s) in the principle, then providing a *worked example* of an application of the causal principle in a work setting.

TRAINEE'S LEARNING OBJECTIVE: You will learn how to state the principle used to predict the stopping distance of a braking vehicle and use this stopping distance principle and a worked example to compute the distance covered by the vehicle that is stopping from the moment the brakes are applied until it comes to a stop.

In a lesson on the maintenance of vehicle brakes, the learner is being asked to learn the following "stopping distance" principle that predicts the amount of distance covered by a braking vehicle.

First, state the principle clearly in cause-and-effect terms. Then describe a problem from the trainee's work setting that the principle can solve and give a worked example of how to apply the principle to solve the problem.

Stopping Distance Principle
Distance in feet = [(initial speed + final speed) / 2] x time

Instructional Design to Teach a Principle
(continued)

State a problem from the trainee's work setting that the principle can solve. Follow the problem statement with a *worked example* of how to apply the principle to solve the problem.

The learner has seen the principle stated and is now being asked to solve a problem asking for the amount of distance covered by a specific braking vehicle.

Problem to Solve: Imagine that your vehicle is traveling 50 feet per second (73 miles an hour) and is slowed down at a constant rate in 20 seconds when you apply the brake. Use the distance principle to determine how far your vehicle moved after the brake was applied.

Instructional Design to Teach a Procedure

A procedure is a clear and complete, step-by-step, "how to" description of the actions and decisions necessary for an individual to learn how to do something.

DESIGNER'S LEARNING OBJECTIVE: You will learn how to design instruction for a procedure.

TRAINEE'S LEARNING OBJECTIVE: You will learn how to change the brake shoes on a vehicle.

You want to teach learners how to change brake shoes. You start by creating a step-by-step text or narrative description of how to change the most common type of brake shoes.

Accompany the text description of each step with a picture of the step being performed or the result of performing the step.

Step 1: **Raise and safely support the vehicle, then remove the front wheels. Work on one wheel at a time until you become familiar with this type of vehicle.**

Siphon fluid out of master cylinder to prevent overflow

Step 2: **Expose the brake pads by removing the bolts that hold the cover over the brake drum and siphon some fluid out of the master cylinder to prevent brake fluid overflow.**

Remove bolts on brake drum cover

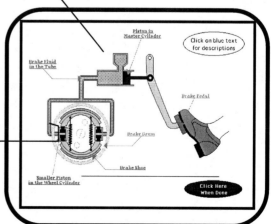

Instructional Design for a Worked Example to Teach a Procedure

Worked examples are clear and complete "how to" descriptions of the actions and decisions necessary to use a procedure to solve a problem.

DESIGNER'S LEARNING OBJECTIVE: You will learn how to design a worked example in order to demonstrate for trainees how to use a principle to solve a problem.

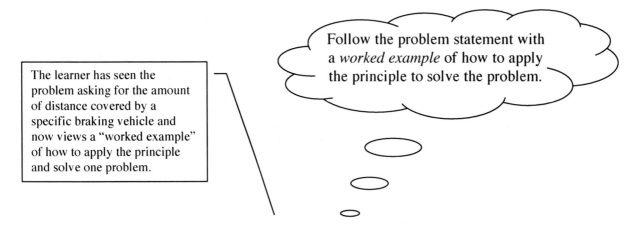

The learner has seen the problem asking for the amount of distance covered by a specific braking vehicle and now views a "worked example" of how to apply the principle and solve one problem.

Follow the problem statement with a *worked example* of how to apply the principle to solve the problem.

Worked Example of the solution to the problem "Your vehicle is traveling 50 feet per second (73 miles per hour) and you slow it down at a constant rate in 20 seconds by applying your brake. How far did your vehicle move after you applied the brake?" You are applying the following principle to solve this problem: "Distance = [(initial speed + final speed)/2] x time"

Step 1: Add the initial speed (73 miles an hour) and the final speed (zero, in this case)
73 + 0 = 73 miles an hour
Step 2: Divide the product of Step 1 (73 miles per hour) by 2
73 / 2 = 36.5
Step 3: Multiply the product of Step 2 by the time (20 seconds)
36.5 x 20 seconds = 730 feet
Step 4: The solution is that your vehicle would have traveled 730 feet before it stopped.

Instructional Design for Giving Feedback During Practice

When learners make a mistake that must be corrected, interrupt with a statement of the goal, describe their positive progress toward the goal, and ask them to reconsider the step they just completed in order to achieve the goal.

DESIGNER'S LEARNING OBJECTIVE: You will learn how to design feedback that can be given in a distance learning setting to trainees who are practicing the application of a principle to solve a work problem.

The learner has seen a "worked example" of how to apply the stopping distance principle to solve one problem. Now the learner has been given another work-related problem to solve, and you are designing corrective and supportive feedback to give as the learner solves the problem.

A mistake has been made, but feedback should not focus on the student or the mistake but instead on the goal and finding a different step or strategy to replace the one that is not achieving the goal.

Please solve this problem: "Your vehicle is traveling 65 miles per hour and you slow it down at a constant rate in 16 seconds by applying your brake. How far did your vehicle move after you applied the brake?" You are applying the following principle to solve this problem: "Distance = [(initial speed + final speed)/2] x time" If you want to see the worked example for this type of problem, click on the example icon.

Learner's solution:
Step 1: 65 + 0 = 65

Step 2: 65 / 2 = 36.5

The learner has made a mistake since 65/2 = 32.5. The mistake may have happened because the learner used the product of the division from the worked example and so needs corrective feedback.

Instructional Design for Giving Feedback During Practice
(continued)

DESIGNER'S LEARNING OBJECTIVE: You will learn how to design feedback that can be given at a distance for learners who have made a mistake while attempting to apply a principle and a worked example to solve a problem.

The learner has seen a "worked example" of how to apply the stopping distance principle to solve one problem. Now the learner has been given another work-related problem to solve, and you are designing corrective and supportive feedback to give as the learner solves the problem.

A mistake has been made—the student apparently copied the solution to Step 2 from the worked example, but feedback should not focus on the student or the mistake but instead on the goal and finding a different strategy to replace the one that is not achieving the goal.

Learner's solution:
Step 1: $65 + 0 = 65$

Step 2: $65 / 2 = \mathbf{36.5}$

Feedback:
The first part of the solution is correct.
The goal of Step 2 is to divide 65 by 2.
Check the answer to Step 2 and try again.

**Strategies Based on Increasing Learner Motivation:
Encouraging Active Engagement and Persistence—Supporting
Learner *Confidence* and *Mental Effort***

Where possible, insert information that helps learners increase their confidence in their proficiency for the skills they are learning by pointing out their strengths by reminding them of their successful mastery of components of the skill. Increase mental effort by pointing out that they thought carefully about what they were doing. One way to insert "confidence and mental effort information" is when you are giving feedback on their practice performance. Increased confidence leads to greater persistence and less distraction or delay when learning. Increased mental effort causes learners to think carefully before solving problems.

The learner has seen a "worked example" of how to apply the stopping distance principle to solve one problem. Now she has been given a number of work-related problems to solve and you are designing motivational feedback to give her confidence as she continues to solve problems and learn. You stress the **NOVEL** nature of the problem she is asked to solve.

Please solve this _new_ problem: "Your vehicle is traveling 65 miles per hour and you slow it down at a constant rate in 16 seconds by applying your brake. How far did your vehicle move after you applied the brake?" You are applying the following principle to solve this problem: "Distance in feet = [(initial speed + final speed)/2] x time" If you want to see a worked example for this type of problem, click on the example icon.

Learner's solution:
Step 1:   65 + 0 = 65
Step 2:   65 / 2 = 32.5
Step 3:   32.5 x 16 = 520 feet

**Feedback:
Your answer is correct. You have solved three of these problems accurately. You have a strong ability for this _novel_ kind of problem. You seem to think carefully about what is required to solve it before you begin.**

Strategies Based on Increasing Learner Motivation:
Encouraging Active Engagement and Persistence—Pointing Out the *Value* of a Skill

Where possible, insert information that helps learners value what they are learning by pointing out the personal and team benefits of knowledge and skills to be learned and the drawbacks of not learning or inadequate learning. Two ways to insert "value information" are when you are describing the reasons for a lesson or giving feedback during practice. More value for a task leads to greater persistence and less distraction during learning.

DESIGNER'S LEARNING OBJECTIVE: You will learn how to design instruction where your trainees will value the information you are presenting, feel confident about their ability to learn, and persist and invest their maximum mental effort to learn it despite the distractions they are experiencing in a distance learning context.

In this lesson you will learn how to change brake shoes quickly, and effectively. This skill is in great demand everywhere.

Personal benefit

Your proficiency at this skill will have a positive impact on the efficiency rating of your motor pool team and on your own performance assessment. You will also be preventing accidents.

Team and personal benefit

Drawbacks of not learning

Avoid Distracting Animated Pedagogical Agents or Attention-Directing Devices

When attempting to draw a learner's attention to a specific word or part of the screen, use subtle, simple techniques such as underlining, bold words, color blocks, or arrows. Avoid animated figures that move and point with accompanying noises and/or music.

DESIGNER'S LEARNING OBJECTIVE: You will learn how to design lessons that direct trainees' attention to critical elements in an instructional display by using the least distracting visual and sound techniques.

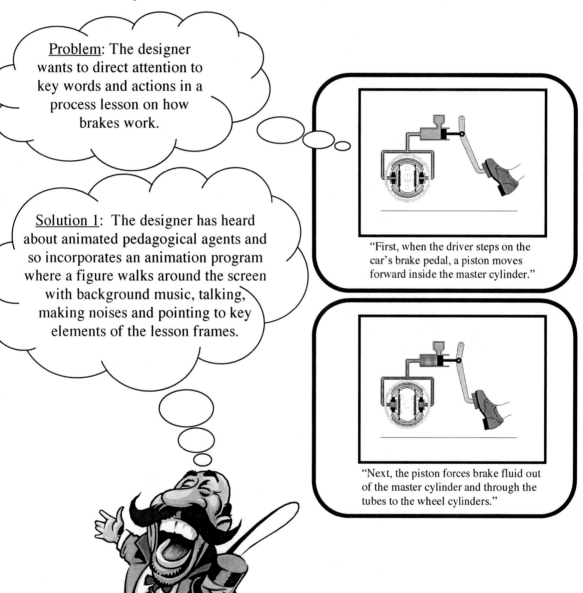

Problem: The designer wants to direct attention to key words and actions in a process lesson on how brakes work.

Solution 1: The designer has heard about animated pedagogical agents and so incorporates an animation program where a figure walks around the screen with background music, talking, making noises and pointing to key elements of the lesson frames.

"First, when the driver steps on the car's brake pedal, a piston moves forward inside the master cylinder."

"Next, the piston forces brake fluid out of the master cylinder and through the tubes to the wheel cylinders."

Avoid Distracting Animated Pedagogical Agents or Attention Directing-Devices (continued)

Problem: You want to direct attention to key words and actions in a process lesson on how brakes work.

"First, when the driver **steps** on the car's brake pedal, a piston **moves forward** inside the master cylinder."

Best Solution: Use the Signaling Principle (see Mayer) and in either text or narration, provide an **outline sentence** (describe the sequence in a process or procedure), **highlighting** (bold font on the key words), and use **pointer words** (such as first, second, etc.) to draw attention without overloading your learners.

"Next, the piston **forces** brake fluid out of the master cylinder and through the **tubes** to the wheel cylinders."

Animated agents are visually interesting but they often distract learners from the key points you are trying to teach.

CHAPTER 4

ASSESSMENT STRATEGIES GUIDELINES' LESSON

Zenaida Aguirre-Muñoz, Jia Wang, and Eva L. Baker
University of California, Los Angeles

Abstract

Baker, Aguirre-Muñoz, Wang, and Niemi (2005) in their chapter in *What Works in Distance Learning: Guidelines* (O'Neil, 2005) presented 11 strategies for assessment. This chapter presents concrete examples of these strategies in the context of developing an assessment to measure knowledge about brake repair and replacement. The chapter opens with how to begin the assessment development process, starting with validity considerations, identifying the targeted cognitive demands, and ensuring domain representation of the assessment. Then, strategies for test specification, scoring, reliability, reporting, formative assessment, and specification of cut scores for certification tests are applied to an automotive braking system domain. Finally, formative and summative evaluation strategies are applied to a distance learning training program for the domain.

Summary

How can you improve the technical quality and validity of assessments used in a distance learning course or training program? In this section, assessment strategies will be illustrated in the context of obtaining information about an individual's knowledge about automotive brake repair and replacement for the purpose of improving upon that knowledge through instruction.

The first strategy is focused on the process of building validity evidence. This process begins by clearly stating test purpose(s), then collecting evidence in support of the legitimacy and accuracy of the intended purposes. Five key assessment characteristics are presented, as well as potential sources of that evidence.

The second strategy centers on the need to describe the cognitive demands of the assessment and on delineating both the domain-dependent and domain-independent cognitive demands. The strategy that follows deals with ensuring adequate sampling of items or tasks that are representative of the domain to be assessed.

The test specification strategies spell out what kinds of information should be included to guide the test designer's attention. Scoring strategies are then applied to both choice-response and performance-based assessments.

Reliability is another aspect of assessment with which designers should be concerned. Examples of scores that have high and low reliability are provided, as well as a list of factors that can influence scores, for example, rater bias, item ambiguity, sampling of items, etc.

It is necessary then to report on the technical quality of the assessment. A sample table of contents of a technical report is provided. Reporting should include comparisons such as performance in relation to particular goals, standards, or overall competency areas. Attention must be paid to the appropriateness of the form of reporting for different audiences or stakeholders.

Formative and summative evaluation strategies are then applied to the distance learning program. The evaluation must be focused by formulating specific questions to address. For summative evaluation purposes, a sound test development process should be followed to increase credibility and robustness of data.

Validity Strategies

Guideline: Validity is the degree to which appropriate inferences, conclusions, or decisions can be made from test results and depends fundamentally on the purpose for which the test is being used.

The process of **building validity evidence** begins by clearly stating test purpose(s), which are closely tied to the content or skill being taught or the educational objectives.

Objectives:	To help students understand (1) conceptual knowledge (e.g., a cause-and-effect model of a braking system) and (2) factual knowledge (e.g., the characteristics of each component in the model), and (3) to help students create and evaluate conceptual knowledge (e.g., revise and critique a cause-and-effect model of a braking system).
Assessment Purposes:	(1) The assessment will indicate the learner's growth in conceptual understanding and factual knowledge of a braking system.
	(2) The assessment will indicate the learner's ability to create and evaluate conceptual knowledge of a braking system.
	(3) The assessment will be given during instruction and indicate to the instructor the areas in which the learner needs additional support.

Validity Strategies
(continued)

Once the intended inferences, conclusions, or decisions are clearly stated, **evidence is accumulated** to support their legitimacy and accuracy.

VALIDITY EVIDENCE FOR FORMATIVE ASSESSMENT
OF BRAKE AND REPAIR LESSON

	Key Assessment Characteristics	Evidence Source
Essential for all assessments	1. Items are within the specified domain	Expert test review Studies that examine the degree to which certain explanatory concepts account for performance
	2. Items comprising the assessment fully represent the domain	Expert test review Studies that examine how well the content of the test samples the concepts/skills about which interpretations are to be made
	3. Performance that is not relevant to the domain is not tested	Studies that examine sources of measurement error
	4. Assessment is fair to identifiable subgroups of examinees	Examination conditions Expert test review Studies that compare performance between subgroups of examinees and involve an examination of the impact of interactions between examinee characteristics and variables related to test performance
Essential for formative assessments	5. Assessment is sensitive to instruction	Studies that compare performance between well-trained examinees and less knowledgeable examinees

Cognitive Demands Strategies

Guideline: Assessment specifications should explicitly reference both the models of cognitive demand in the task (e.g., knowledge understanding or problem solving) and the cognitive requirements of desired performance in the specific content area.

COGNITIVE ANALYSIS OF BRAKE REPAIR AND REPLACEMENT ASSESSMENT

TARGETED CONCEPT/SKILL FOR ASSESSMENT: Automotive Brake Repair and Replacement

TARGETED COGNITIVE DEMANDS OF TASK: The assessment should elicit basic knowledge about a car's brake system:

Domain-dependent cognitive demands:

- Identify key components of a brake system

- Comprehend the functions of the components of a brake system

- Understand how brake systems work

- Perform proper part replacement

- Knowledge of procedures for diagnosing needed repairs

Domain-independent cognitive demands:

- Troubleshoot to identify source(s) of malfunction

Domain Representation Strategies

Guideline: Tests must contain adequate sampling of items or tasks that are representative of the content domain to be assessed.

Adequate sampling begins with a detailed description of the domain. Often, the target domain is specified in the curriculum statements and content standards. A matrix can be used to identify what concepts/skills should be covered by the assessment.

Numbers represent the total number of items that target each construct.

Targeted Concept/Skill	Total No. of Items	Content Domain Constructs/Topic Areas									
		1	2	3	4	5	6	7	8	9	10
Braking system components	10	2	2	2	2	2					
Component functions	15						2	3	3	5	2
Part replacement procedures	10	5	5								
Malfunction troubleshooting	15			5	3	2	3	2			
Performance	12	2	2	2	2					2	2
Total	62	9	9	9	7	4	5	5	3	7	4

Once the domain is defined and items are developed, experts use this information to match specifications and test item features. Experts identify:

- Gaps
- Overrepresentation
- Content errors

Test Specification Strategies

Guideline: Prior to item, test, or task development, test specifications should be prepared to guide the test designers' attention to key elements of the test such as test purposes, intellectual skills, content, and format of the test.

TEST PURPOSE:	Evaluation of mechanic's knowledge and skills
TARGETED CONCEPT/SKILL:	Automotive Brake Repair and Replacement
TARGETED COGNITIVE DEMANDS:	The assessment should elicit basic knowledge about a car's brake system:

Domain-dependent cognitive demands:
(80% of the items)

(1) Identify key components of a brake system

(2) Comprehend the functions of the components of a brake system

Specifications should indicate the proportion of items that should target domain-dependent and domain-independent items.

(3) Understand how brake systems work

(4) Perform proper part replacement

(5) Knowledge of procedures for diagnosing needed repairs

Domain-independent cognitive demands:
(20% of the items)

(1) Troubleshoot to identify source(s) of malfunction

Test Specification Strategies
(continued)

CONTENT *(partial list)*:
Assessments must contain adequate sampling of items or tasks that are representative of the content domain to be assessed.

(1) Components of the master cylinder (e.g., metal cylinder, piston)
(2) Functions of master cylinder components
(3) Direction of the flow of hydraulic fluid
(4) Relationship between master cylinder and wheel cylinders
(5) Brake pad replacement

ITEM FORMAT:
Low-level skills are better assessed using traditional methods for assessment (e.g., choice-response items), whereas higher level knowledge and skills are more easily assessed using *alternative and/or performance assessments.*

A major disadvantage is that choice-response is susceptible to guessing and decontextualized knowledge assessment.

Low-level content-dependent knowledge (1, 2, 3) will be assessed using either choice-response or diagram completion. Knowledge of conceptual understanding will assessed using open-ended or performance tasks.

TEST FORMAT:
Performance assessment (e.g., simulations) requires examinees to construct their own responses to questions or prompts. The assessment imitates or creates the real context in which the examinees can demonstrate their knowledge and skills.

The assessment should include two components. The first component is comprised of choice-response items for each key content area for a total of 50 items. The second component is comprised of 12 performance assessments, one assessing brake pad replacement and the others assessing troubleshooting to identify source of malfunction.

Scoring Strategies

Guideline: A scoring framework should include information on the measurement scale, scoring criteria, performance descriptions of each criterion at each point on the scale, and sample responses that illustrate the various levels of performance.

CHOICE-RESPONSE ASSESSMENTS

With choice-response assessment, the scoring procedure consists of (a) specifying the answer key for each item, (b) a rule for adding up the scores, and (c) the actual scoring of the assessment. The scoring, typically done by machines, is fast, economical, and relatively free of scoring error.

Key				
1. A	6. D	11. A	16. D	21. B
2. D	7. A	12. C	17. C	22. A
3. C	8. C	13. B	18. C	23. D
4. B	9. A	14. B	19. B	24. D
5. A	10. A	15. A	20. A	25. B

Calculating Scores

Scores for each of the subskills are calculated by adding the total number correct for each of the subskills.

Overall scores are calculated by adding the total number correct.

Disadvantage: Choice-response assessment is susceptible to guessing and decontextualizes knowledge assessment.

Scoring Strategies
(continued)

PERFORMANCE-BASED ASSESSMENTS

Performance-based assessment (e.g., essay items or simulations) requires examinees to construct their own responses to questions or prompts. The assessment imitates or creates the real context in which the examinees can demonstrate their knowledge and skills.

Performance-based assessment requires human judgment. The scoring is usually done by raters and requires careful selection of raters and detailed design and administration of training and scoring sessions.

PERFORMANCE TASK RUBRIC

Performance Levels	Qualities of Performance		
	Content	Procedures	Timeliness
Exceeds Expectations	4	4	4
Meets Expectations	3	3	3
Approaching Expectations	2	2	2
Severe Gaps in Performance	1	1	1

Measurement Scale (1-4)

PERFORMANCE SCORING GUIDELINES

	Content
Exceeds Expectations	• Response demonstrates understanding of cause-and-effect models • Response describes an efficient method for troubleshooting • Identifies the source of malfunction

Performance Description

Reliability Strategies

Guideline: A reliable test should give accurate and similar scores from one occasion to another, from one form of a test to another, and from one rater to another.

High Reliability: The scores for the system components construct are consistent in that for the most part, the scores are the same from one time to the next time. (T = time)

Low Reliability: There is little consistency in the scores for component functions, and therefore one cannot make reasonable inferences about students' knowledge of component functions.

STUDENT PERFORMANCE FOR TEST 1

	System Components		Component Functions	
	T1	T2	T1	T2
Ryan	8	9	7	14
Jose	6	7	14	8
Lisa	9	8	15	9
Ana	9	9	7	13
Gus	3	4	5	15

Like validity, reliability is a conclusion based on evidence that is gathered in a variety of ways. The emphasis is placed in the reliability of scores and not of the tests themselves. Scores are influenced by many factors including:

Rater bias	Sampling of items	Examinee health	Test-taking skills
Item ambiguity	Test interruptions	Mood	Anxiety
Clarity of directions	Scoring	Motivation	Fatigue
Luck	Observer differences	Observer bias	General ability

Reporting Strategies

Guideline: Information on technical quality is needed, including studies of reliability, appropriateness of the test for the particular content and user group, and validity interpretations of the results.

The purpose(s) of testing should be clearly articulated and form the basis of the approach to collecting and reporting the technical quality of the assessment.

To judge the utility of the findings or standards, it is essential to report the magnitude of the measurement error and the level of accuracy given the examinee sample.

Proving validity evidence on the link between a new assessment and existing measures increases the meaning and utility in terms of the test results.

The extent to which an assessment is instructionally sensitive is particularly important for formative assessments.

TECHNICAL REPORT

CONTENTS

Reporting Strategies
(continued)

Reporting should include comparisons such as performance in relation to particular goals, standards, or overall competency areas. Attention must be paid to the appropriateness of the form of reporting for different audiences or stakeholders. This example is intended for the instructor and learner.

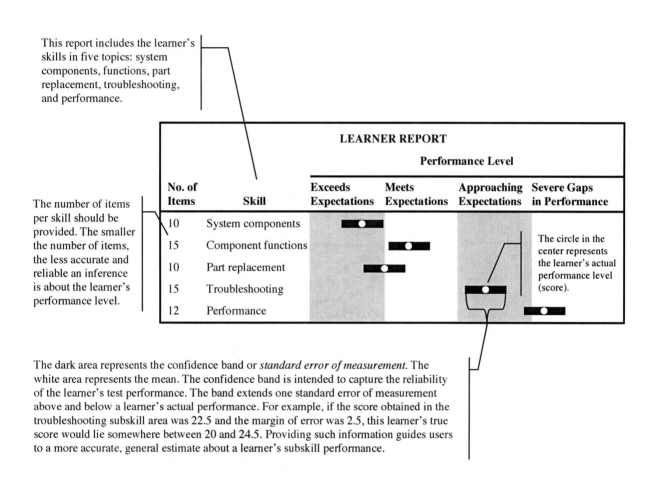

This report includes the learner's skills in five topics: system components, functions, part replacement, troubleshooting, and performance.

The number of items per skill should be provided. The smaller the number of items, the less accurate and reliable an inference is about the learner's performance level.

The circle in the center represents the learner's actual performance level (score).

The dark area represents the confidence band or *standard error of measurement*. The white area represents the mean. The confidence band is intended to capture the reliability of the learner's test performance. The band extends one standard error of measurement above and below a learner's actual performance. For example, if the score obtained in the troubleshooting subskill area was 22.5 and the margin of error was 2.5, this learner's true score would lie somewhere between 20 and 24.5. Providing such information guides users to a more accurate, general estimate about a learner's subskill performance.

Appropriate levels of technical language, graphs, and acceptable documentation of technical data will vary for different audiences.

Formative Assessment Strategies

Guideline: Tests given during instruction should provide information for feedback and motivation to the learner and guide the program to provide needed help. In addition, such information gives the instructional designer information about program strengths and weaknesses.

To assess knowledge of the basic components of the master cylinder, examinees can be provided with a diagram of a master cylinder and asked to label each of the components and describe their respective functions.

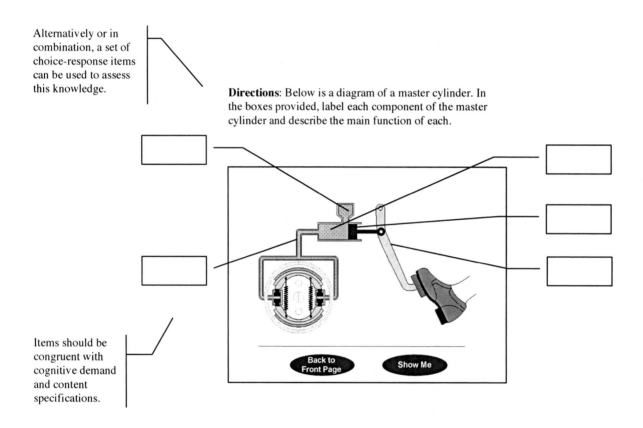

Alternatively or in combination, a set of choice-response items can be used to assess this knowledge.

Directions: Below is a diagram of a master cylinder. In the boxes provided, label each component of the master cylinder and describe the main function of each.

Items should be congruent with cognitive demand and content specifications.

Back to Front Page

Show Me

The feedback to learners is specific to the major skills or knowledge areas being assessed instead of one score that represents their overall understanding of the domain. This provides the learner information about areas of strength and weakness. It also provides instructors with areas to target for additional instruction.

Certification Tests: Cut Score Strategies

Guideline: The specification of the cut score of a certification test should be based on empirical studies that indicate accurate distinctions among levels of performance (for example, acceptable and unacceptable).

Tests for certification are designed to determine whether the core knowledge and skills of a specified domain have been mastered by the candidate. Therefore, prior to test development, a clear statement of the objectives of the test should be prepared.

			LEARNER REPORT			
			Performance Level			
No. of Items	Score	Skill	Exceeds Expectations	Meets Expectations	Approaching Expectations	Severe Gaps in Performance
10	9	System components	●			
15	8	Component functions		●		
10	8	Part replacement	●			
15	8	Troubleshooting		●		
12	9	Performance	●			

The cut score of 40 is based on expert judgment in addition to empirical studies that demonstrated better job performance for those obtaining a score of 40 or better.

Total: 42

Recommendation: Job placement

Formative Evaluation Strategies

Guideline: Formative evaluation provides information that focuses on improvement of an innovation and is designed to assist the developer.

First, **focus the evaluation** by formulating specific questions to address. If the purpose is to understand how to improve an innovation, it is helpful to have a model of how aspects of a program fit together.

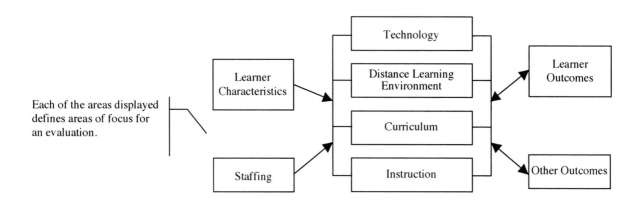

Typical formative evaluation questions: On learner outcomes—How has the introduction of distance learning affected learner outcomes in required courses? How has the introduction of graphical models improved learner understanding of brake systems? On curriculum—How can curriculum goals and expectations for learner performance better meet learner needs? How has the curricular focus on brake repair and replacement improved on-the-job performance? On instruction—What strategies have worked best to support less able learners? On staffing—Which staff members can be used to provide training for others in the use of available technology?

Summative Evaluation Strategies

Guideline: Tests used for summative program evaluation should assist decision makers in their decisions on whether they should select, continue, modify, or drop a program.

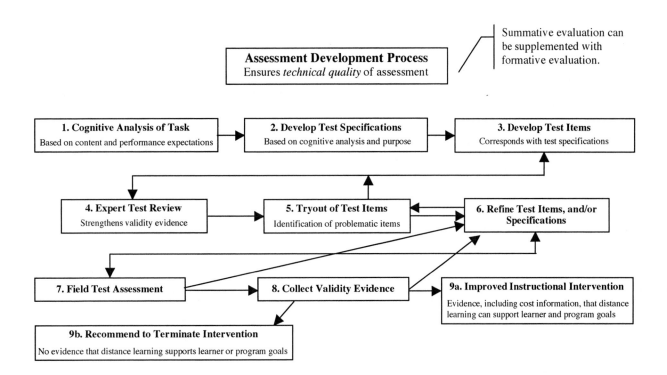

Summative evaluation process: The process starts with a cognitive task analysis (1) that leads to the development of test specifications (2). From the test specifications, test items are developed (3). The test items are reviewed by experts (4), and the review leads to either a tryout of these items (5) or the development of new test items (3). The tryout of test items (5) leads to the refinement (6) and in some cases a new tryout of items (5) and revision of specifications (6). Following the refinement of items (6), the items are field tested (7), which leads to collection of validity evidence (8) and in some cases further refinement of items (6). The validity evidence (8) leads to an adoption decision (9a) or a termination decision (9b).

CHAPTER 5

LEARNING STRATEGIES GUIDELINES' LESSON

Myron H. Dembo and Linda Gubler Junge
University of Southern California

Abstract

Dembo and Gubler Junge (2005) in their chapter in *What Works in Distance Learning: Guidelines* (O'Neil, 2005) presented 12 learning strategies that could aid a learner in a distance learning setting to maximize his or her learning experience. The 12 learning strategies discuss details of text summarization, annotation, visual representations, elaborative interrogation, elaborative verbal rehearsal, generation of higher level questions, outline-formatted notes, test preparation, help seeking, time management, goal setting, and test anxiety reduction. These strategies are applied in this document to learning about brakes. The strategies are written from the learner's perspective.

Summary

What can students do to improve their chances of success in a distance learning setting? Individuals who take responsibility for their own learning, by controlling the factors that influence their learning, tend to be more successful learners. Individuals who exhibit these active behaviors are called self-regulated. Key self-regulatory skills are briefly summarized in this section and are then followed with examples of how a self-regulated individual might employ each strategy when learning about brakes. We will reference Clark's instructional strategies lesson (see chapter 3) in this chapter.

Text Summarization

Students who summarize readings comprehend and recall more than those who do not. The process of summarizing text after reading provides students the opportunity to both generate meaning and monitor understanding. When summarizing, students make connections between words, sentences, paragraphs, and concepts in the text in addition to making connections to personal knowledge and experience.

Annotation

Annotating text while reading improves comprehension. Annotation takes less time than traditional strategies like rereading, outlining, and taking notes, and it is more useful than highlighting because it is an active process, not a passive one. It requires connecting to prior knowledge and experience, as well as elaboration of ideas. When students annotate a text, they actively interact with it much as they would when conversing with another individual.

Visual Representations

Visual representation of text material is helpful in improving comprehension of complex material. Reading involves two processes: comprehension and retention. Just because textbook material is comprehended does not mean that it will be retained. Additional steps such as visual representations improve comprehension of detailed material, and also improve retention and performance.

Elaborative Interrogation

Students who interact with texts by forming and answering questions based on readings show greater comprehension. Elaborative interrogation means that students interact with a text by forming and answering questions based on the reading, thereby turning what was a passive reading process into an active one.

Elaborative Verbal Rehearsal

When students explain a concept or idea out loud, either to another person or to an imaginary audience, performance on recall and recognition measures is enhanced. The idea that the teacher often learns more than the students is embodied in the elaborative verbal rehearsal strategy, wherein students verbally explain, either to another person or to an imagined audience, material that was learned in a lecture or in a reading assignment.

Generation of Higher Level Questions

When thought-provoking questions about learned material are generated by students, deeper understanding and higher academic performance results. If higher level question stems are used in student-generated questions, then comprehension improves. Higher level questions are thought-provoking questions that require synthesis, elaboration, application, and prediction of ideas (i.e., What are the strengths and weaknesses of…? How does…affect…? Why is…important? Compare…and…with regard to…, etc.; see King, 1992). These questions can be formed before, during, and/or after reading.

Outline-Formatted Notes

If outline formatted notes are taken and periodically reviewed, then comprehension increases. The number of ideas included in notes is positively related to test performance. In other words, the more extensive the notes individuals have, the better their chances are of performing well on academic measures.

Test Preparation

If students adjust their study strategies to match testing demands, then test scores are higher. For example, the requirements of a history test may be different from the requirements of a math test. The history test may focus on memory for names and dates, whereas the math test may require application of concepts. Similarly, the test in one history class may have different demands than the test in another class covering the same material. Memory-focused tests have different cognitive demands than do application type tests.

Help Seeking

Active learners who are motivated to achieve tend to seek help when it is needed from social (i.e., teachers or classmates) or nonsocial sources (i.e., written sources), or both, when faced with complex and/or difficult tasks.

Time Management

Students who use their time efficiently are more likely to learn and/or perform more successfully than students who do not have good time management skills. Successful students know how to manage their time in order to learn and accomplish necessary tasks. Self-regulated students know how to manage their time because they are aware of deadlines, how long it will take to complete each assignment, and their own learning processes.

Goal Setting

If individuals have specific challenging goals, then academic performance is enhanced through directed attention, increased effort, and persistence. As individuals select and pursue goals, they are able to progress, gain feedback, and self-monitor their progress. In addition, goals can help individuals become more self-motivated.

Test Anxiety

Students' test anxiety can be reduced, and often test performance increased, by using a variety of educational interventions, such as systematic desensitization, relaxation training, and cognitive-behavioral treatments.

Cognitive-behavioral treatments involve a number of treatments that focus on the notion that thoughts cause feelings. Thus, it is believed that if one can change his or her own thoughts, then feelings can be changed, and finally, a change of behavior will occur. One such cognitive-behavioral treatment is The Rational Emotive Approach developed by Albert Ellis (1998), who proposed that irrational thinking follows an "A-B-C-D-E" model of development. "A" stands for an activating event. "B" stands for a belief (irrational) that follows the activating event. "C" stands for the consequence of the irrational negative thinking. "D" stands for disputing the irrational/helpless belief that followed the activating event and should be aimed at replacing the maladaptive beliefs with an adaptive and realistic belief. "E" is the new effect—that is, the improvement in the way that one feels and acts after actively disputing the maladaptive belief that followed the adversity.

The Lesson

We illustrate the use of different learning strategies for the unit on brake repair and replacement by demonstrating what a self-regulated learner would say to himself or herself while interacting with the content in the lesson. It is important to note that not all of these strategies would be used to learn each objective in the unit. The learner would select the strategies that best help him or her learn the content and assist in the performance of required skills.

Text Summarization

Guideline: Students who summarize readings comprehend and recall more than those who do not.

Our self-regulated learner says:

"Okay, I just read the first page about brakes (Clark, Concepts) and want to make sure that I understand how a brake works as explained on this page—so, I am going to see if I can summarize in my own words what it said. I'll write the summary at the bottom of my page of notes:

"When I step on the brake, hydraulic fluid is forced out of the cylinder into a tube which forces the brake linings against my wheel, slowing the car to a stop.

"I'm going to check back in the reading and see that I got the terms right and understood everything…Okay…the piston is what applies the pressure and pushes out the fluid. I should include that. I could insert it above or below. I'll just add it onto what I wrote at the end…

"When I step on the brake, hydraulic fluid is forced out of the cylinder into a tube which forces the brake linings against my wheel, slowing the car to a stop. The moveable piston forces the fluid out of the cylinder as I apply pressure with my foot."

This strategy is very useful when learning factual information needed to learn concepts.

Annotation

Guideline: Annotating text while reading improves comprehension.

Our self-regulated learner says:

"While I was reading about the brake master cylinder (Clark, Concepts) I wrote '5 main brake parts' in the margin next to the 5 words in bold. I also formed some questions pertinent to what I read that I thought I might need to be able to answer during an assessment. Some of the questions I wrote are: 'How does a vehicle stop? And...Identify the various parts and explain their functions.' I then underlined and/or drew arrows to where I could find the answers to my questions. This process helps me to make sure that I have understood what I read and that I have gotten the main point of the reading; it also helps me to prepare for tests and other assessments. Something especially helpful when forming questions to answer is to use the words from the heading of the section—those words normally help me extract the main point of what I just read. That's why I normally use the heading itself to help me form a question like 'How does the brake master cylinder work?' "

5 main
brake parts

Identify the
various parts
and explain
their functions.

How does a
vehicle stop?

CONCEPT: Brake Master Cylinder—How does the b.m.c. work? **Definition**: A <u>metal cylinder</u>, containing a small, <u>**moveable piston**</u> that is **connected to the <u>brake pedal</u>** on one side, and a <u>**metal tube**</u> that extends to the brake cylinder on the other side. The master cylinder is **filled with <u>hydraulic brake fluid</u>**. <u>As you apply pressure on the brake pedal with your foot it **forces** the small movable piston in the brake master cylinder to push the **hydraulic fluid into the metal tube** on the other side of the cylinder to force the brake linings against your wheel drum to slow down or stop your car.</u>

This learning strategy is effective for all types of learning—concepts, processes, principles, and procedures.

Visual Representations

Guideline: Visual representation of text material is helpful in improving comprehension of complex material.

Our self-regulated learner says:

"I have found that creating visual representations helps me to better understand complex information. I have been learning about braking systems, and have tested my understanding several times by drawing on my own in my notebook what I just read about and looked at. I then label the various parts and as I do so explain to myself what each part does. When I did it the first time, I wrote the functions of each part below the name in the diagram (Clark, Processes). In addition to the diagrams of the braking systems that I drew, I made flow charts so that I could remember the order in which things happen when braking and stopping a vehicle. You can see what I did below…"

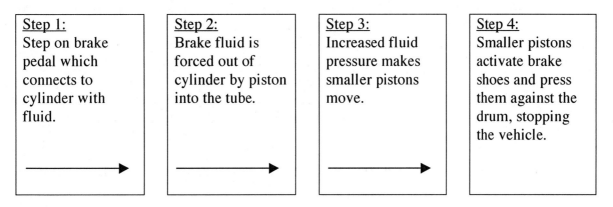

| Step 1: Step on brake pedal which connects to cylinder with fluid. | Step 2: Brake fluid is forced out of cylinder by piston into the tube. | Step 3: Increased fluid pressure makes smaller pistons move. | Step 4: Smaller pistons activate brake shoes and press them against the drum, stopping the vehicle. |

"Creating visual representations is especially helpful to me when the material is complex and when there is no visual provided. However, even when there are visuals provided, producing my own helps me to understand the processes more completely by focusing me on detail."

This learning strategy is effective for all types of learning—concepts, processes, principles, and procedures.

Elaborative Interrogation

Guideline: Students who interact with texts by forming and answering questions based on readings show greater comprehension.

Our self-regulated learner says:

"While I read, I look for the main point by turning the headings into questions and then underlining the answers to my questions. For example, 'Brake Master Cylinder' becomes 'How does the brake master cylinder work?' (Clark, Processes). While I read, I also ask myself how, what, and why questions frequently in order to make sure that I understand what I read, and also to make sure that I am paying attention as I read and not zoning out. For example, when I read about the various brake parts I briefly paused and asked myself, 'What are the various parts?' I then looked again at the names and counted to see that there were 5. I then wrote '5 main brake parts' in the margin next to the 5 words in bold. I also formed some questions pertinent to what I read that I thought I might need to be able to answer during an assessment. Some of the questions I wrote are: 'How does a vehicle stop?' and…'Draw, label, and explain the brake master cylinder.' I then underlined and/or drew arrows to where I could find the answers to my questions. As I read I continue to ask myself questions; for example, 'Why is that true?' is what I might ask myself when reading about the smaller pistons activating brake shoes and stopping the vehicle. I would answer and connect to things that I have previously learned about friction and resistance. By asking myself questions while I read, I am able to make sure that I'm paying attention and that I'm understanding while I connect to prior knowledge.

"I compile the annotations in my book and create notes *with questions* that I use to prepare for tests."

This learning strategy is effective for all types of learning—concepts, processes, principles, and procedures.

Elaborative Verbal Rehearsal

Guideline: When students explain a concept or idea out loud, either to another person or to an imaginary audience, performance on recall and recognition measures is enhanced.

Our self-regulated learner says:

"When I am studying for a test, I normally recruit a friend or a roommate to quiz me with the questions that I have produced in my notes and book. When I was getting ready for the test on the brake master cylinder (Clark, Concepts, Processes, Principles), I had my roommate, Ron, help me. I gave him my notes with all my questions and answers. He asked me things like…

- What are the 5 main brake parts?
- How does a vehicle stop?
- Draw, label, and explain how the brake master cylinder operates.
- Identify and explain the different parts of the equation associated with the Stopping Distance Principle.

"When Ron has the same course, I will quiz him right back, using his questions. This is especially helpful, because sometimes he has questions that I don't, and I find that I missed something that he picked up—and vice versa."

This learning strategy is effective for all types of learning—concepts, processes, principles, and procedures.

Generation of Higher Level Questions

Guideline: When thought-provoking questions about learned material are generated by students, deeper understanding and higher academic performance results.

Our self-regulated learner says:

"Here are examples of questions that I use when studying (Clark, Concepts, Processes, Principles):

1. What are the main functions of each of the 5 main brake parts?
2. How does a vehicle stop?
3. How does the brake master cylinder work? Draw, label, and explain the various parts.
4. What are the various concepts in the Stopping Distance Principle equation?

"Though a question such as 'What are the 5 main brake parts?' can easily be answered by simply listing off 5 words, and does not require much explanation or synthesis of ideas, a question like 'How does a vehicle stop?' requires deeper understanding and synthesis of ideas. To answer such a question I would have to not only to know the various components, but also show an understanding of what they do and how they do it. That is why I primarily use higher level questions. They require me to go beyond rote memorization to meaningful learning of concepts, processes, and principles. When I use questions like this as I read and study, I find that I have a deeper understanding and find myself predicting test questions that I encounter later."

This learning strategy is effective for all types of learning—concepts, processes, principles, and procedures.

Outline-Formatted Notes

Guideline: If outline-formatted notes are taken and periodically reviewed, then comprehension increases.

Our self-regulated learner says:

"When I am studying on my own—as I have been while learning about brakes—my notes become especially important in helping me to bring different ideas and concepts together, pick out the main points, and prepare for tests (Clark, Concepts, Processes). My notes are very organized. I take notes in outline form; I use headings to indicate main points and indent underneath the main point so that I can keep everything together that goes together and also see relationships between related things. I also skip lines in between main points to keep the various concepts clearly separated, and I make sure to include definitions of terms. I then write questions in the left column to test my understanding of the individual concepts and to knit the various concepts together. I underline the answers to my questions in the body of the notes on the right, and that is all I underline. My underlining serves this specific purpose. You can see an excerpt from my notes below…

Identify and define the 5 main brake parts?	I. Brake Master Cylinder
	    A. metal cylinder—contains the fluid
	    B. hydraulic brake fluid—flows from cyl through tube
	    C. brake pedal—connects to cyl and presses out fluid
	    D. metal tube—connects cyl to brk pads + smaller pistons
	    E. movable piston—connects brk pedal + cyl, pushes fluid

How does a vehicle stop?	II. Braking Stages
	    A. Step on brk pedal which connects to cyl with fluid.
	    B. Brk fluid is forced out of cyl by piston into the tube.
	    C. Increased fluid pressure makes smaller pistons move.
	    D. Smaller pistons activate brk shoes + press them against the drum, stopping the vehicle.
	
	 Summary:
	    When I step on the brk, hyd fluid is forced out of the cyl into a tube which forces the brk linings against my wheel, slowing the car to a stop. The movable piston forces the fluid out of the cyl as I apply pressure with my foot.

"I like to use as many abbreviations as possible in order to make the process quicker. That is why I wrote 'brk' for brake and 'cyl' for cylinder. I also commonly use '+' for and, and 'b/c' for because. I also write a summary to see if I can put things into my own words, and will commonly add visual representations as well to my notes to increase my understanding."

This learning strategy is effective for all types of learning—concepts, processes, principles, and procedures.

Test Preparation

Guideline: If students adjust their study strategies to match testing demands, then test scores are higher.

Our self-regulated learner says:

"When I began studying for the test on brakes, I was thinking that it would be multiple choice and that I would consequently need to be prepared to identify the correct answer; so I studied using flashcards that I made with the names of the various parts on one side and the definition of what they did on the other side. I was also looking over my notes a little bit to see if I could remember the various braking stages and procedures for changing brake pads, but I mostly focused on quizzing myself with the flashcards…

"However, yesterday I talked to a buddy who just took this, and he told me that the tests are not multiple choice, but performance with a short essay. In other words, I have to be prepared to do more than just recognize the correct answer. For the essay, I need to be able to explain things and give my own examples to illustrate points I am making. I need to demonstrate deeper understanding of concepts, processes, principles, and procedures associated with brakes. That is why I am now relying more on using the questions that I generated in my annotations and notes, and am having my roommate, Ron, quiz me when he has time—and when he doesn't have time, I quiz myself orally answering the questions as thoroughly as I can, trying not to look too much at my notes. I have also been practicing writing the answers down after drafting a mock test with the questions that I am predicting will be on the exam.

"More importantly, I will need to show that I can apply my knowledge and make it useful by doing things like changing the brake pads (Clark, Procedures). This weekend during my off time, I plan to practice on my friend's car. I will prepare for this procedure by first reviewing the different parts and functions of the braking system by using the diagram in my notes. Next, I will review the two steps in the procedure."

This learning strategy highlights the need to determine the type of learning or performance required before selecting the manner of preparation for the criterion measure.

Help Seeking

Guideline: Active learners who are motivated to achieve tend to seek help when it is needed from social (i.e., teachers or classmates) or nonsocial sources (i.e., written sources), or both, when faced with complex and/or difficult tasks.

Our self-regulated learner says:

"I am having difficulty attaining two of the goals related to a car's braking system—how to solve a worked example and how to change brake shoes. I located a book in the library about brake repair and replacement to supplement what I learned in the multimedia lesson. This book should help me to clarify concepts and understand things better. Also, I plan to study in a group with two other students. Before the group meets, I asked each member to bring their notes to the meeting, and be prepared to (a) review the goals for the lesson, (b) identify each member's ability to attain each of the goals, (c) diagnose the reasons why a group member is unable to attain a goal, (d) provide remedial instruction for members having specific problems with goals, and (e) develop and answer additional test questions concerning the content."

Help seeking can vary greatly in distance learning depending on the nature of student difficulty. In this example, we illustrate two ways to seek help—obtaining nonsocial resources (e.g., additional reading material) and using peers for collaborative study. Other sources of help seeking could include librarians, technical support, and instructor assistance.

Time Management

Guideline: Students who use their time efficiently are more likely to learn and/or perform more successfully than students who do not have good time management skills.

Our self-regulated learner says:

"Because I am responsible to independently work and complete this unit on brakes, I want to make sure that I use my time wisely in order to complete what I need to on time. The last couple of days I have been spent time hanging out talking to my buddies that I could have better spent studying. I think that I was underestimating the amount of time that I would need to read the material, annotate the text, summarize what I had read, and produce questions that help me to both monitor my understanding and prepare to be assessed. I will need to set up a routine and a schedule for myself using goals…

"OK, tonight I want to finish the section dealing with the Stopping Distance Principle. I want to read the pages, annotate the text, summarize what I have read, and produce additional questions for studying. The section is not very long, so reading and annotating should take me about…15-20 minutes; however, I will probably need to put in another 15-20 minutes to work the problems and try generating one of my own. Then taking notes, summarizing, and generating additional questions will probably take me another 20 minutes—so I will need to block out an hour of time to study this section tonight…"

This learning strategy is useful for the management of time for large amounts of material and preparation for an examination over the material.

Goal Setting

Guideline: If students have specific challenging goals, then academic performance is enhanced through directed attention, increased effort, and persistence.

Our self-regulated learner says:

"I need to make sure that I am getting things done in a timely way, and am understanding what I'm reading, so I'm going to set some goals for the week.

"By the end of the week, I will:

1. Diagram all five defining characteristics of a brake master cylinder.
2. Describe verbally what happens at each stage to make a brake master cylinder work.
3. State the Stopping Distance Principle that predicts the amount of distance covered by a braking vehicle.
4. Use the Stopping Distance Principle to solve a problem asking for the amount of distance covered by a specific braking vehicle.
5. Describe the steps about how to change brake shoes next to the picture of the brake master cylinder."

This learning strategy is useful for all types of learning and can increase learner self-motivation for the complete lesson (see also Clark, Strategies Based on Increasing Learner Motivation).

Test Anxiety

Guideline: Students' test anxiety can be reduced, and often test performance increased, by using a variety of educational interventions, such as systematic desensitization, relaxation training, and cognitive-behavioral treatments.

Our self-regulated learner says:

"Word problems have always stressed me out. I really hate these problems. Okay…I need to deal with this anxiety so that I can get through this, understand the concept, and solve the problem successfully. I'll use the Ellis method I learned about…

> A (activating event)—encountering the challenging problem.
> B (the irrational or helpless belief that follows the event)—"I was never good at solving these types of problems."
> C (consequence)—"I feel anxious and believe that I cannot learn the material."
> D (disputing irrational beliefs)—"OK…what I did in the past should not relate to what I can do now. I know that if I read the material and review the information, I can learn this stuff."
> E (new effect)—"I am a little unsure of myself, but I am not going to let my past influence my future success as a student."

This learning strategy is useful for all types of learning when an individual is faced with anxiety-provoking situations.

CHAPTER 6

SELF-REGULATION STRATEGIES GUIDELINES' LESSON

Harold F. O'Neil and San-hui Chuang
University of Southern California

Abstract

O'Neil and Chuang (2005) in their chapter in *What Works in Distance Learning: Guidelines* (O'Neil, 2005) presented self-regulation strategies that could aid a learner in a distance learning setting to maximize his or her learning experience. The self-regulation strategies instantiated from a trainee perspective here include goal specificity, setting process and outcome goals, self-evaluation, self-monitoring, self-questioning, and effort allocation. These strategies are shown with explanations in detail. The strategies are general strategies rather than task specific. However, the task of learning about brakes is used in some lessons as a specific example. The strategies are written from the learner's perspective.

Summary

One important element that helps to improve online learning effectiveness is a learner's self-regulation strategies. In this chapter, self-regulation strategies that help learners succeed in the learning tasks are presented with detailed explanations. Six strategies are illustrated: goal specificity, setting process and outcome goals, self-evaluation, self-monitoring, self-questioning, and effort allocation.

The first lesson is on goal specificity. Learners learn better with specific performance goals that with general goals such as "Do you best." For example, when learning about how brakes work, learners are encouraged to set their goals to be as specific as possible: "After studying the lesson, I will be able to know how to diagram all five defining characteristics of a brake master cylinder," rather than "After studying the lesson, I will be able to know about a brake master cylinder."

In addition to goal specificity, there is a difference between setting process goals and setting outcome goals. Students who set process goals initially and then shift to outcome goals learn better than those who adhere to process goals only; in addition, students who adhere to process goals learn better than those who adhere to outcome goals only. The best self-regulation strategies set several process goals along the way and then move on to a final outcome goal.

Self-evaluation is third strategy offered in this chapter. During the process of learning, students who self-evaluate their learning results regularly are conscious of their own progress and performance in learning. This awareness makes them learn better academically than those who do not self-evaluate their learning results.

In addition to self-evaluation, self-monitoring and self-questioning are also researcher-recommended self-regulation strategies for learners. Learners who periodically monitor their own learning processes, by checking what they know and what they do not know yet, perform better academically than those who do not monitor their own learning. A self-monitoring protocol is provided for learners' reference.

Learners who ask themselves questions about the learning content while learning perform better academically than those who do not. A list of generic sample questions is provided in the lesson.

The last strategy offered is a strategy based on effort allocation. Self-regulated learners strategically allocate effort according to what they know and what they do not know about the content to be learned. They learn better because effort allocation gives learners a chance to evaluate what they know or do not know, and this information can help learners change the allocation of their effort after a period of time at the task.

Goal Specificity

Guideline: Learners learn better with specific performance goals than with general goals, such as "Do your best."

Our self-regulated learner says:

"I need to set learning goals that are as specific as possible because specific goals help me learn better than general goals. An example of a general goal is: After studying the lesson, I will be able to know how a brake works.

"I should be able to define more specific learning goals, such as these:

1. After studying the lesson, I will be able to diagram all five defining characteristics of a brake master cylinder.

2. After studying the lesson, I will be able to describe verbally what happens at each stage to make a brake master cylinder work.

3. After studying the lesson, I will be able to state the Stopping Distance Principle that predicts the amount of distance covered by a braking vehicle.

4. After studying the lesson, I will be able to use the Stopping Distance Principle to solve a problem asking for the amount of distance covered by a specific braking vehicle.

5. After studying the lesson, I will be able to describe the steps about how to change brake shoes next to the picture of the brake master cylinder."

Strategies Based on Setting Process and Outcome Goals

Guideline: Students who set process goals initially and then shift to outcome goals learn better than those who adhere to process goals only; in addition, students who adhere to process goals only learn better than those who adhere to outcome goals only.

Our self-regulated learner says:

"I need to set several process goals in the initial stage of learning and then as the lesson draws to an end, I should shift to final outcome goals. My final outcome goal is: I am able to use the knowledge that I learned to redesign the brakes in my car and make them more effective. Before reaching the final outcome goal, I defined several process goals that would lead to the final outcome goal. Here are my process goals and final outcome goals.

"Process goals:

1. After the first time I study the lesson, I will be able to diagram all five defining characteristics of a brake master cylinder.

2. After the second time I study the lesson, I will be able to describe verbally what happens at each stage to make a brake master cylinder work.

3. After the third time I study the lesson, I will be able to state the Stopping Distance Principle that predicts the amount of distance covered by a braking vehicle.

4. After the fourth time I study the lesson, I will be able to use the Stopping Distance Principle to solve a problem asking for the amount of distance covered by a specific braking vehicle.

5. After the fifth time I study the lesson, I will be able to describe the steps about how to change brake shoes next to the picture of the brake master cylinder.

"Outcome goals:

1. After the end of the lesson, I will be able to troubleshoot a braking problem. For example, if I step on the brake pedal in my car but the brakes don't work, I will be able to figure out what has gone wrong.

2. After the end of the lesson, I will be able to use the knowledge that I learned to redesign the brakes in my car and make them more effective; that is, to reduce the distance needed to bring the car to a stop."

Strategies Based on Self-Evaluation

Guideline: Students who self-evaluate their learning results regularly are conscious of their own progress and performance in learning perform better academically than those who do not.

Our self-regulated learner says:

"I need to self-evaluate my learning results regularly. I need to be conscious of my own progress and performance in learning. An example of a self-evaluation tool that I can use will be a strategy checksheet. For example, after learning how to diagram all five defining characteristics of a brake master cylinder, I can use the following strategy checksheet and content understanding checksheet to evaluate my own learning performance.

"Self-Evaluation Strategy:

"As I learn the five characteristics of a brake master cylinder, I checked my understanding by

relating what I was learning to what I know;

picturing each characteristic in my mind;

comparing and contrasting each characteristic;

summarizing what I understand;

asking myself questions.

"Summary of my strategy use:

_____

_____

"Content understanding checksheet:

Description of five different characteristics

Comparison of five different characteristics

Diagram of five different characteristics"

Strategies Based on Self-Monitoring

Guideline: Students who periodically monitor their own learning progress by checking what they know and don't know perform better academically than those who do not monitor their own learning.

Our self-regulated learner says:

"I need to monitor my learning activities regularly. I do so by recording my learning progress on a self-monitoring protocol. I will get extra feedback from the self-monitoring protocol and use it to improve my learning outcomes.

"Here is an example of a self-monitoring protocol, which I adapted from Lan (1996)."

	Knowledge elements	Text time and Exposure		Discussion time and Exposure		Total time and Exposure		Self-efficacy for element
Lesson 1	Five defining characteristics	A	B	A	B	A	B	C
Lesson 1	The mechanism of how a brake cylinder works	A	B	A	B	A	B	C
Lesson 1	The Stopping Distance Principle	A	B	A	B	A	B	C
Lesson 1	The steps of changing brake shoes	A	B	A	B	A	B	C

Time and Exposure

In the box with letter A, students put down how much time they spend on the element. In the box with letter B, students put down how many times they expose themselves to the element. In the box with letter C, students fill in a number between 1 and 10 to indicate how self-efficacious they are in understanding or solving the problems relating to the concept.

Strategies Based on Self-Questioning

Guideline: Learners who question themselves about the learning content while learning perform better academically than those who do not.

Our self-regulated learner says:

"I need to self-question my own learning When I question myself about what I have learned and I am able to answer questions that I have developed, I will have a sense of achievement and, in turn, will be more willing to continue learning. On other hand, when I am unable to answer the questions I have developed for myself, I need to change my way of learning so that I will be more successful in learning the content.

"Here are some of my self-questioning questions. For example, after learning how to diagram all five defining characteristics of a brake master cylinder, a question such as: How do these defining characteristics relate to what I learned before? will help me to integrate the new information with materials previously studied. A question such as: How do these five characteristics contribute to the mechanism of how a brake works? will help me to think more deeply about how these characteristics interact with each other. When I am unable to find out the answers, I might resort to remedial solutions, such as reviewing the lesson or reviewing my notes, to get a more complete and deeper understanding.

"Here is a list of generic sample questions according to King (1994, p. 171).

What is a new example of …?

How could … be used to …?

What would happen if …?

Explain why …

Explain how …

What is the meaning of …?

Why is … important?

Compare … and … with regard to …

What is the difference between … and … ?"

Strategies Based on Effort Allocation

Guideline: Self-regulated learners strategically allocate effort according to what they know and what they do not know about the content to be learned. They learn better because effort allocation gives learners a chance to evaluate what they know or do not know and, in addition, possibly change their allocation of effort if necessary after a period of time at the task.

Our self-regulated learner says:

"From what I know and what I do not know about the content, I need to make a decision about how I allocate my effort. If I know the content very well, it means my effort allocation is correct and appropriate. If after studying, I still did not understand the content completely, I might need to re-allocate my effort so that I will be more successful in learning the content.

"Here are some processes that I use for effort re-allocation, based on Zimmerman (1998).

"Goal setting:

When specific and quantifiable goals are set daily and weekly, is the effort allocated enough to finish the goals? If the goals are not being met, find out whether more effort needs to be invested or the goals have to be changed.

"Time management:

Examine daily and weekly scheduling to see what and where the available studying time is spent.

"Self-consequences:

Is studying a priority over fun and pleasure? Is learning the content a must before resting and enjoyment?

"Environment structuring:

What is the physical studying environment? Is the environment suitable for quiet, secluded studying?

"Help seeking:

Is there a study partner? Will a study partner help? When there is difficulty in understanding the content, can a learner seek help? Help might come from someone more knowledgeable, an expert, books, Internet and libraries. A self-regulated learner will have comprehensive help-seeking resources and will seek help so that rather than being stuck at one point, more time and effort can be spent on the task."

CHAPTER 7

MANAGEMENT STRATEGIES GUIDELINES' LESSON

Edward J. Kazlauskas
University of Southern California

Abstract

This chapter of the Guidelines' "Lessons" provides an expansion of the content dealing with management strategies to support distance learning efforts. The topics that are addressed cover the following: a policy framework, administrative structure, and appropriate procedures and interventions; the technical support environment; quality assurance; library and information systems and services; content management; and student support services. These topics were the guidelines by Kazlauskas (2005) in *What Works in Distance Learning: Guidelines* (O'Neil, 2005).

This chapter includes an expansion of the original Guidelines 1–6. The last three Guidelines (7–9) are not included in this chapter. Guideline 8 (Learner Characteristics) and Guideline 9 (Instructional Design) overlap with guidelines provided in other chapters. In regard to Guideline 7 (Instructor Competency), there appears to be a general gap in the guidelines regarding the topic of instructors and teaching. Given the nature of management strategies for distance learning, the format of this Lesson differs from previous Lessons.

Summary

For each distance learning management strategy, a guideline is provided from O'Neil (2005). In each guideline a task scenario is presented that places the guideline into an action mode. These actions are as follows: provide the principles/rationale of good policy development, the components inherent in a policy plan, the considerations associated with an administrative structure, and a complement of policies and procedures; outline the components of a technical infrastructure that addresses the technical architecture, the choice of a learning management approach, the ongoing system management, and future planning; outline general quality measures in such areas as organizational support, course development, teaching/learning, course structure, student support, instructor support, evaluation/assessment and outcomes, and the steps to be taken to assure that the standards are met; build a library and information system that supports a distance learning program by providing options for information services, and plan for the integration of the system and services as components of the learning space; monitor and be proactive regarding the developments in content management and in the re-use and interoperation among learning systems; and provide an appropriate learner support environment with assistance in counseling, scheduling and registration, problem solving, mentoring, delivery of course materials, and maintenance of appropriate records and transcripts. Options for implementing the task scenario are presented under each guideline. Typically these provide a detailed discussion of specific activities that can be employed to implement the strategy. Examples include selecting and implementing a learning management system, employing adherence to various standards, using electronic online journals, monitoring the development of learning content management systems, and implementing a student enrollment and advisement subsystem. After each guideline there is a list of references, a glossary of terms, and a checklist of strategies appropriate for each guideline. The various checklists can be used by different categories of individuals, such as internal policymakers, managers, and external contractors. The checklists can be used as a guide for distance learning program planning efforts, for the preparation of a request for a proposal for some aspect of distance learning, and as guidelines for a vendor's development effort.

Strategies Based on Policy Framework and Administrative Structure

1. Guideline:

A policy framework, administrative structure, and appropriate procedures and interventions should be developed to support distance learning efforts.

2. Task Scenario:

Provide the principles/rationale of good policy development, the components inherent in a policy plan, the considerations associated with an administrative structure, and the complement of policies and procedures needed for an effective distance learning effort.

3. Personnel:

Internal

4. Options:

4.1 Develop a Policy Framework

There is a multiplicity of issues associated with developing policy for a distance learning effort. The scale of options ranges from a policy-free environment (decisions made on a case-by-case basis) to that of a policy-restricted environment (where decisions on issues are made in accordance with established policies). Policy clarifies issues of potential concern or litigation, and policy provides a guide for individual action in distance learning efforts (Meyer, 2002). The need for policy development is documented in the literature, and such policy is essential to a successful distance learning effort in terms of physical, programmatic, and organizational impact. It is also noted that it is essential to have the input of stakeholders and that issues identified in internal and external needs assessment be resolved during the planning stage. The overall challenge is to determine how to design, implement, and operate a distance learning program (Levy, 2003). Policy involves both general and specific components, with a typical structure consisting of a mission statement, then a vision statement, then a plan with goals, objectives, strategies, and measures of attainment and assessment of success factors.

Components of policy have been identified in the literature, such as those that address the barriers that need attention in any planning effort (Cho & Berge, 2002), and the identified constructs that organize barriers to distance learning (Muilenburg & Berge, 2001). Bunn (2001) identified the student-related issues, instructional issues, and organizational issues that are reflected in a four stage process: planning stage, development stage, implementation stage, and control stage. Compora (2003) outlined a distance education administrative operative model that consists of a set of issues for consideration. Phipps and Merisotis (2000) identified a list of benchmarks for quality distance education.

A synthesis of these models and the incorporation of other elements generates the following list of components for policy development consideration: administrative-related (administrative structure, organizational change, approval systems, budget and finance, marketing and recruitment, coordination); technical-related (infrastructure and expertise); content-related (curriculum, delivery methods); instructor-related (instructor compensation and time, instructor involvement and training); student-related (social interaction and quality, support services); ethics-related (copyright, intellectual property, scholastic dishonesty and plagiarism); and quality control (assessment, evaluation, effectiveness). While the incorporation of all these components may not be necessary in every context, a more complete complement of policies provides a robust approach to the management of distance learning

4.2 Develop an Administrative Structure

The administrative structure needs to present a management team that has a shared vision, is involved in strategic planning, and can support the organizational change that is inherent in distance learning efforts (Cho & Berge, 2002). There is the need to have personnel who can address the wide spectrum of needs, such as finance and budgeting, marketing, program development, program sustainability, instructional systems design, human performance technology (HPT), instructional and graphics design, design and delivery process management, implementation, technology management and support, site management, instructor and user training and support, and evaluation. Various types of organizational structures exist with the underlying principles being to utilize a type of structure that enhances management for the particular organization and to meet the larger organizational goals. Prestera and Moller (2001) noted four different structures: a distance learning program in which courses are developed by individuals within a unit (e.g., an academic department in a university); a distance learning unit entity working within an organization (e.g., a university or company); a distance learning institution which has as its sole purpose the delivery of distance learning; and a distance learning consortium, an alliance of several units or institutions sharing responsibilities. Job structures can consist of functional, divisional, project, matrix (workers have two immediate supervisors, one for their area of expertise and another being the course project manager), virtual (use of temporary skilled workers and external entities, such as consultants), and consultant team models (content experts, e.g., instructors working with internal design and technology consultants).

4.3 Develop Appropriate Policies and Procedures
Many policies and procedures are necessary for an effective distance learning effort. These cover the many topics already identified as components of distance learning policy. A list of these is included as part of the Checklist of Strategy Elements Based on Policy Framework and Administrative Structure.

5. References:

Bunn, M. D. (2001). Timeless and timely issues in distance education planning. *The American Journal of Distance Education, 13*(1), 55-67.

Cho, S. K., & Berge, Z. L. (2002). Overcoming barriers to distance training and education. *United States Distance Learning Association Journal, 16*(1). Retrieved July 11, 2002, from http://www.usdla.org/html/journal/JAN02_Issue/article01.html

Compora, D. P. (2003). Current trends in distance education: An administrative model. *Online Journal of Distance Learning Administration, 6*(2). Retrieved July 5, 2003, from http://www.westga.edu/~distance/ojdla/summer62/compora62.html

Levy, S. (2003). Six factors to consider when planning online distance learning programs in higher education. *Online Journal of Distance Learning Administration, 6*(1). Retrieved July 5, 2003, from http://www.westga.edu/~distance/ojdla/spring61/levy61.html

Meyer, K. A. (2002). Does policy make a difference? An exploration into policies for distance education. *Online Journal of Distance Learning Administration, 5*(4). Retrieved July 5, 2003, from http://www.westga.edu/~distance/ojdla/winter54/Meyer_policy_54.htm

Muilenburg, L. Y., & Berge, Z. L. (2001). Barriers to distance education: A factor analytic study. *The American Journal of Distance Education, 13*(2), 7-22.

Phipps, R., & Merisotis, J. (2000). *Quality on the line: Benchmarks for success in internet-based distance education.* Washington DC: Institute for Higher Education Policy.

Prestera, G. E., & Moller, L. A. (2001). Organizational alignment supporting distance education in post-secondary institutions. *Online Journal of Distance Learning Administration, 4*(4).

Retrieved July 18, 2002, from
http://www.westga.edu/~distance/ojdla/winter44/presetera44.html

6. Glossary:

Human performance technology (HPT): HPT uses a wide range of interventions that are drawn from many other disciplines including behavioral psychology, instructional systems design, organizational development, and human resources management. As such, it stresses a rigorous analysis of present and desired levels of performance, identifies the causes for the performance gap, offers a wide range of interventions with which to improve performance, guides the change management process, and evaluates the results. A description of this performance improvement strategy emerges. Human: the individuals and groups that make up our organizations. Performance: activities and measurable outcomes. Technology: a systematic and systemic approach to solve practical problems. *What is Human Performance Technology?* Retrieved August 8, 2003, from http://www.ispi.org/

7. Checklist:

Checklist of Strategy Elements Based on Policy Framework and Administrative Structure (check yes/no)	Yes	No
Develop a Policy Framework		
1. Is there a policy framework/distance learning plan?		
2. Does the plan incorporate a mission and vision statement?		
3. Does the plan incorporate goals and objectives?		
4. Does the plan identify strategies?		
5. Does the plan address measures of attainment and assessment of success?		
6. Did the plan utilize the needs assessment approach?		
7. Does the plan incorporate administrative-related components (administrative structure, organizational change, approval systems, budget and finance, marketing and recruitment, program sustainability, coordination)?		
8. Does the plan incorporate technical-related components (infrastructure and expertise)?		
9. Does the plan incorporate content and content delivery-related components (curriculum, design, delivery methods, vendor management)?		
10. Does the plan incorporate instructor-related components (instructor selection, instructor compensation and time, instructor involvement and training)?		

	Yes	No
11. Does the plan incorporate student-related components (social interaction and quality, support services)?		
12. Does the plan address ethics-related components (copyright, intellectual property, academic dishonesty and plagiarism)?		
13. Does the plan incorporate quality control components (assessment, evaluation, effectiveness)?		
Develop an Administrative Structure		
14. Is there a management team that has a shared vision?		
15. Is the management team involved in strategic planning?		
16. Can the management team support the organizational change that is inherent in distance learning efforts?		
17. Does the administrative structure include personnel (in-house and external) that can support the wide spectrum of needs of a distance learning effort?		
18. Does the administrative structure enhance management for the particular organization?		
Develop Appropriate Policies and Procedures		
Are there administrative policies and/or procedures that address each of the following:		
19. Marketing?		
20. Recruitment?		
21. Curriculum, e.g., procedures and criteria to select and develop courses, and procedures for course approval?		
22. Delivery methods, e.g., the course management system to be utilized and whether multiple delivery modes will be employed?		
23. Types of student-instructor-media communication, interaction, assignment characteristics?		
24. Library and information resource services?		
25. Technical infrastructure?		
26. Technical support for instructors and students?		
27. Program and course support services?		
28. Student costs, e.g., tuition and fees, and financial aid?		
29. Student services, e.g., advisement, enrollment, transfer and articulation?		
30. Library and resource access?		
31. Student training and support?		
32. Selection process of instructors?		
33. Instructor work issues, e.g., compensation and workload?		
34. Instructor training and support?		

	Yes	No
35. Intellectual property rights?		
36. Copyright?		
37. Academic dishonesty and plagiarism?		
38. Quality criteria, e.g., procedures and criteria and metrics for evaluation?		
39. Measures of cost and operating efficiency?		

Strategies Based on Technical Support Environment

1. Guideline: Provide an appropriate technical support environment for distance learning.

2. Task Scenario: Outline the components of a technical infrastructure that addresses the technical architecture, the choice of a learning management approach, the ongoing system management, and the future planning needed for an effective distance learning effort.

3. Personnel: External

4. Options: 4.1 Develop the Technical Capability

A first step in developing technical capability is to generate a technology plan that outlines requirements. In general, such a plan would focus on various issues, including the need to manage the cost and the return on technology investment, and to increase productivity. Typically, there is the need to integrate solutions across the organization by interfacing and connecting, as needed, with multiple internal administrative systems and any appropriate external systems, for example, personnel, computer account system, registration and ERP (Enterprise Resource Planning) systems. McGraw (2001) states the goal of technical capability as the need to integrate legacy learning, enterprise applications, online learning, and emerging tools using a standards-driven technical architecture that facilitates linkage and global access. At a more specific level, the technical capability includes system, application and network implementation and management; a solid base of technology and personnel talent; appropriate logistical, process, and development support; system monitoring to ensure reliability and performance; robust environmental control, power, and security systems; disaster recovery plans; and a scalable architecture that would support usage growth. The aforementioned items are equally important whether there is an internal technology infrastructure or whether it is outsourced to a technology provider(s), such as Collegis (http://www.collegis.com) or IBM Business Consulting Services (http://www.ibm.com/services/bcs/us), which, for example, supplies the hardware and managed hosting service for eArmyU.

4.2 Select and Implement Learning Management

A major aspect of developing a technical infrastructure is in determining the technologies to be employed with the concern for integrating existing and future online learning elements, and matching content to delivery, whether that be, for example, Web-based training, interactive TV, use of a course management system

(CMS) or learning management system (LMS) (covered in more depth under Strategies for Quality Assurance), or a customized, developed system. Paramount considerations are to select systems that foster interactivity, facilitate information presentation and communication, and interface with the existing technical infrastructure.

Today, a major aspect of developing the technical support environment is the conscious effort of selecting a learning management system. Evangelisti (2002) identified the must-have features of an LMS. These include supporting virtual courses, as well classroom courses that operate in a blended mode; integrating with human resources or student registration systems; managing the myriad of administrative activities; allowing for content integration (e.g., from third-party providers); and adhering to standards, such as AICC (covered in more depth under Strategies for Quality Assurance). Enhanced value is achieved by including assessment features, skills management, collaborative components, and content management capabilities. Brandon-Hall Inc. (2007) continue their reporting on the LMS marketplace and presented a list of elements to be considered including such items as scalability, interoperability, learner interface, classroom training management, competency and certification management, content development and management, testing and assessment, reporting, standards, customization, and support. An examination of learning technology products themselves generates an additional extensive list of possible features to consider, such as ability to post announcements, course content, assignments, vitae, readings, and Web-links; course management; calendaring; chat-rooms and threaded discussions; documentation, online support and manuals; email functionality; individual user and group management; testing and assessment; online grade-book; and course and user statistics.

The learning technology provider arena is an active marketplace with many players, such as Blackboard (http://www.blackboard.com), WebCT (http://www.webct.com), Saba (http://www.saba.com/english/index.asp), and others. A representative list of learning management systems can be found at EduTools Course Management Systems (http://www.edutools.info/index.jsp) and a comprehensive list can be found at Brandon-Hall Inc. (2007).

Learning technology may be hosted internally, or for those who do not have the technical infrastructure to locally deliver and manage the software, clients can be provided with the latest software applications and complete system management services across a wide area network or via the Internet, from a secure data center. Blackboard Application Service Provider (ASP) Solutions is an example of such a managed e-Education solution (https://www.educase.edu/ir/library/pdf/ERB0210.pdf).

Learning systems are constantly improving. For example, the current development of WebCT's Vista e-learning system is built to support multiple organizations, or departments within one organization, in a single installation, while allowing each entity to operate autonomously. Each entity is able to maintain local control of the system to preserve individual branding, support unique objectives, and facilitate content sharing (http://www.webct.com). Another example is the move of learning system providers to participate in the effort to develop systems that comply with SCORM Standards (covered in more depth under Strategies for Quality Assurance).

4.3 Develop Ongoing System Management
In general terms, in any ongoing maintenance there should be the utilization of standard management practices associated with operating computing and network services, including addressing such components as maintenance, server space, redundancy, load balancing, documentation, and technical training. Of importance is system support in terms of help desk operations, including call-in, email service, and development of FAQs. In any technology-based system there is the need to assure for integrity and validity of information and to guarantee system reliability and security.

4.4 Plan for Improvement
Not only is there the concern for ongoing technology management; there is also concern for planning for the future. Constant monitoring is required for upgrades/improvements to hardware, software, system, networks, and services. Future planning also includes considering the incorporation of advanced technologies, such as wireless, new multi-user collaborative and interactive tools, and intelligent agency into the distance learning program; investigating open source initiatives built to O.K.I. and IMS specifications (covered in more depth under Strategies for Quality Assurance), for example, Coursework (http://coursework.stanford.edu); examining the integration of a CMS or an LMS to a framework for interconnectivity whereby content from various activities are placed into one site, such as course materials, research projects, work activities (that is, an enterprise portal with applications and interface customized and adaptive to the user); and facilitating the linkage with content management systems.

5. References:

Brandon-Hall Inc. (2007). Reference to a full, extensive online database, LMS KnowledgeBase 2007. Retrieved May 10, 2007, from http://brandon-hall.com/publications/lmskb/lmskb.shtml

Evangelisti, D. (2002). The must-have features of an LMS. *Learning Circuits.* American Society for Training and Development. Retrieved July 20, 2002, from http://www.learningcircuits.org/2002/mar2002/evangelisti.html

McGraw, K. L. (2001). E-learning strategy equals infrastructure. *Learning Circuits.* American Society for Training and Development. Retrieved July 20, 2002, from http://www.learningcircuits.org/2001/jun2001/mcgraw.html

6. Glossary:

AICC (The Aircraft Industry CBT Committee): AICC has developed a set of highly regarded guidelines that have been used to measure quality in the development, delivery, and evaluation of CBT (computer-based training) and related training products. The guidelines are fairly general and applicable to most industries. *AICC FAQ.* Retrieved August 8, 2003, from http://www.aicc.org/pages/aicc_faq.htm

Blended mode: Learning events that combine aspects of online and face-to-face instruction. E-Learning Glossary. *Learning Circuits.* American Society for Training and Development. Retrieved August 8, 2003, from http://www.learningcircuits.org/glossary.html

Course management system (CMS): A course management system, or CMS, is usually software that has capabilities in three areas: (a) design interface and content assembly; (b) the facilitation of communication and collaboration; and (c) course management support. [Note that this acronym is also used for a content management system, also known as a CMS, which refers to a system used to manage the content of a Web site.] Typically, a CMS consists of two elements: the content management application (CMA) and the content delivery application (CDA). The CMA element allows the content manager or author, who may not know Hypertext Markup Language (HTML), to manage the creation, modification, and removal of content from a Web site without needing the expertise of a Webmaster. The CDA element uses and compiles that information to update the Web site. The features of a CMS system vary, but most include Web-based publishing, format management, revision control, and indexing, search, and retrieval. *Course Management Systems (CMS).*

Retrieved May 10, 2007, from
http://www.educause.edu/ir/library/pdf/DEC0302.pdf

ERP (Enterprise Resource Planning): A set of activities
supported by application software that helps a company manage
such core parts of its business as product planning, parts
purchasing, inventory management, order tracking, and customer
service. Can also include modules for finance and human resource
activities. The deployment of an ERP system can involve
considerable business process analysis, employee retraining, and
new work procedures. E-Learning Glossary. *Learning Circuits*.
American Society for Training and Development. Retrieved
August 8, 2003, from
http://www.learningcircuits.org/glossary.html

FAQ (Frequently Asked Questions): An informational list, in
question-and-answer format, of common inquiries from users
about a topic or application and standard responses. FAQs appear
on Websites and discussion boards and within desktop
applications. E-Learning Glossary. *Learning Circuits*. American
Society for Training and Development. Retrieved August 8, 2003,
from http://www.learningcircuits.org/glossary.html

IMS (The IMS Global Learning Consortium): IMS has
developed open technical XML-based specifications for
exchanging learning content and information about learners in
learning management systems. *IMS Global Learning Consortium
Inc*. Retrieved July 6, 2003, from http://www.imsglobal.org

Learning management system (LMS): Software that automates
the administration of training. The LMS registers users, tracks
courses, records data from learners, and provides reports to
management. An LMS is typically designed to handle courses by
multiple publishers and providers. It usually doesn't include its
own authoring capabilities; instead, it focuses on managing courses
created by a variety of other sources. E-Learning Glossary.
Learning Circuits. American Society for Training and
Development. Retrieved August 8, 2003, from
http://www.learningcircuits.org/glossary.html

O.K.I. (The Open Knowledge Initiative): O.K.I. is a
collaboration of universities and standards organizations that is
developing open and extensible architecture for interoperability
among learning systems and other enterprise systems. O.K.I. has
established a set of fundamental services that foster
interoperability—for example, Service Interface Definitions,

which, when implemented, have the potential of reducing development efforts, facilitating integration of new modules, and minimizing the need for back-end development efforts for new applications. *The Open Knowledge Initiative*. Retrieved May 10, 2007, from http://www.okiproject.org

Open source: Generally, software for which the original program instructions, the source code, is made available so that users can access, modify, and redistribute it. E-Learning Glossary. *Learning Circuits*. American Society for Training and Development. Retrieved August 8, 2003, from http://www.learningcircuits.org/glossary.html

SCORM (Sharable Content Object Reference Model): SCORM provides specifications that are adapted from multiple sources and user groups and which facilitate the interoperability, accessibility, and reusability of learning content. These specifications are being used by the vendor community, as well as by instructional designers and content developers. *Advanced Distributed Learning*. Retrieved July 5, 2003, from http://www.adlnet.org

XML (Extensible Markup Language): The next-generation Webpage coding language that allows site designers to program their own markup commands, which can then be used as if they were standard HTML commands. E-Learning Glossary. *Learning Circuits*. American Society for Training and Development. Retrieved August 9, 2003, from http://www.learningcircuits.org/glossary.html

7. Checklist:

Checklist of Strategies Based on Technical Support Environment (check yes/no)	Yes	No
Develop the Technical Capability		
1. Is there a technology plan that outlines requirements?		
2. Is there an integrated technology solution?		
3. Can the technology handle legacy learning systems?		
4. Is there a standards-driven technical architecture?		
5. Is there capability in system implementation?		
6. Is there capability in network implementation?		
7. Is there capability in application implementation?		
8. Is there capability in system management?		

	Yes	No
9. Is there capability in network management?		
10. Is there capability in application management?		
11. Is there a solid technology base?		
12. Is there a solid personnel base?		
13. Is there appropriate logistical support?		
14. Is there appropriate process support?		
15. Is there appropriate development support?		
16. Is there adequate system reliability		
17. Is there adequate response time?		
18. Are there adequate levels of system performance?		
19. Is there an adequate level of environmental control?		
20. Is there an adequate power system?		
21. Is there an appropriate security system?		
22. Is there a disaster recovery plan?		
23. Is the architecture scalable to handle future growth?		
Select and Implement Learning Management		
24. Is there a determination of what technologies to employ for distance learning?		
25. Do the selected technologies foster interactivity?		
26. Do the selected technologies facilitate information presentation?		
27. Do the selected technologies foster communication?		
28. Do the selected technologies interface with the existing technical infrastructure?		
29. Do the selected technologies meet established benchmarks?		
Does a learning technology, e.g., CMS or LMS, have the following elements?		
30. Support virtual and blended courses?		
31. Support virtual and classroom management?		
32. Integrate with human resources and/or student registration to authenticate users?		
33. Other users (those not in human resources and/or student registration databases) can be added to the system?		
34. Integrate with other systems, e.g., ERP and other enterprise systems?		
35. Allow for interoperability?		
36. Manage necessary administrative activities?		
37. Adhere to standards?		
38. Support individual and group management?		
39. Allow individual and group customization?		
40. Allow for multiple user levels?		
41. Incorporate a content management system?		

	Yes	No
42. Incorporate content development tools?		
43. Incorporate content management tools?		
44. Allow for text, audio, and video content?		
45. Allow for posting of materials?		
46. Provide a calendaring function?		
47. Link to library and e-reserve systems?		
48. Incorporate email functionality?		
49. Allow for variety of input, e.g., scientific notation?		
50. Utilize collaborative tools, e.g., chat rooms?		
51. Utilize collaborative tools, e.g., threaded discussions?		
52. The ability to import third-party tools?		
53. Incorporate testing and assessment tools?		
54. A variety of question type and response options?		
55. Incorporate skills, competency, and certification management?		
56. Provide a reporting capability?		
57. A function to link electronically to an online grading/notification system?		
58. Provide an online grade-book?		
59. Generate use and user statistics?		
60. The ability to import/export Excel files?		
61. Provide documentation?		
62. Provide online help and support?		
63. A scalable system?		
64. A customizable system?		
65. Appropriate levels of technical support?		
66. Support from vendor for upgrades/migrations?		
67. A vendor product advisory committee?		
68. A migration tool?		
Develop Ongoing System Management		
69. Are standard computing and network management practices employed?		
70. Is there adequate system maintenance?		
71. Is there adequate server space?		
72. Is there appropriate redundancy?		
73. Is there adequate load balancing?		
74. Is there appropriate documentation?		
75. Is there adequate technical training?		
76. Are there a variety of help support options, including help-desk, FAQs, email services, remote login?		
77. Are the help support operations adequate?		

	Yes	No
Plan for Improvement		
78. Are there plans for hardware upgrades and improvements?		
79. Are there plans for network upgrades and improvements?		
80. Are there plans for application upgrades and improvements?		
81. Are there efforts to incorporate advanced technologies to support distance learning?		
82. Is there an effort to examine open source initiatives?		
83. Is there an effort to investigate expansion to an enterprise portal?		
84. Is there an effort to investigate the use of content management systems?		

Strategies Based on Quality Assurance

1. Guideline: In order to assure quality, establish standards for distance learning programs.

2. Task Scenario: Outline general quality measures in such areas as organizational support, course development, teaching/learning, course structure, student support, instructor support, evaluation/assessment and outcomes, and include the steps to be taken to assure that the standards are met.

3. Personnel: Internal

4. Options: 4.1 Develop General Measures
The literature presents a variety of approaches to examining the overall quality of distance learning, although the components identified in the literature are similar in nature. In *Quality on the Line* (Phipps & Merisotis, 2000), a series of benchmarks have been established to measure the quality of distance learning. These benchmarks cover a wide spectrum of topics, including the following: Institutional/Organizational Support (e.g., technology planning, technical delivery reliability, a centralized support system); Course Development (e.g., guidelines regarding minimum standards, technology determined by requirements of learning outcomes, periodic review of instructional materials, and student engagement); the Teaching/Learning Process (e.g., interaction levels with peers and instructors, feedback, use of proper methods of research and evaluation); Course Structure (e.g., advisement regarding distance learning, appropriate course information, library resources, completion expectations); Student Support (e.g., student services information, training and information on resource access and use, technical assistance, responsiveness to student inquiries); Faculty Support (e.g., technical assistance in course development, transition assistance, training and assistance, ethics policies); and Evaluation and Assessment (e.g., multiple methods and application of standards, evaluation of program effectiveness, and review of learning outcomes).

Other reports are similar in scope. The UK Quality Assurance Agency for Higher Education (n.d.) has generated a series of distance learning guidelines that provide a list of characteristics that an institution might be expected to have in place. These guidelines cover such characteristics as the development of an integrated systems approach; the establishment of a program design, approval and review process; the management of program delivery; student development and support; student communication and representation; and student assessment.

Academic institutions typically utilize the accreditation model for quality assurance wherein distance learning is one component of an overall institutional accreditation process. Specific distance learning institutional quality factors are found in some accreditation standards, such as those by the Western Interstate Commission for Higher Education ([WICHE] 2001). The WICHE document identifies best practices for distance learning programs and certificates. The components identified include institutional context and commitment, such as adequate budget, policy statements, and infrastructure; curriculum and instruction, such as academic rigor and use of qualified personnel; faculty support, such as specifying workload levels and compensation adjustments; student support, such as library services and advisement; and evaluation and assessment.

4.2 Employ Standards Adherence

There are multiple developments occurring in the area of standards for distance learning. For example, the Benjamin Franklin Institute of Global Education has an initiative that is focusing on using the International Organization for Standardization (known as ISO; www.iso.ch) as a basis for certification of distance education programs. This approach measures quality in terms of having a quality management system. ISO 9000 is a quality assurance model with a series of system requirements that act as a guide and assist in Quality Assurance Certification (Benjamin Franklin Institute of Global Education, 2003). The Aircraft Industry CBT Committee (AICC) has developed a set of highly regarded guidelines that have been used to measure quality in the development, delivery, and evaluation of CBT and related training products. The guidelines are fairly general and applicable to most industries (http://www.aicc.org). The Learning Technologies Standardization Committee (LTSC) of the IEEE (Institute of Electrical and Electronics Engineers, Inc.) develops technical standards, and recommends practices and guides for learning technology. The LTSC coordinates its efforts with other organizations working on similar learning issues (http://ltsc.ieee.org/).

Considerable work is occurring in the area of specific distance learning technical standards, including IMS, SCORM, and O.K.I. The IMS Global Learning Consortium has developed open technical XML-based specifications for exchanging learning content and information about learners in learning management systems. IMS has released a series of specifications, including those relating to metadata, question and test interoperability, content packaging, learner information, enterprise interoperability, and competency definitions (http://www.imsglobal.org). The Sharable Content Object Reference Model (SCORM) provides specifications adapted from multiple sources and user groups and which facilitate the interoperability, accessibility and reusability of learning content. These specifications are being used by the vendor community, as well as by instructional designers and content developers (http://www.adlnet.org). The Open Knowledge Initiative (O.K.I.) is a collaboration of universities and standards organizations that is developing open and extensible architecture for interoperability among learning and other enterprise systems. They have established a set of fundamental services that foster interoperability—for example, Service Interface Definitions that have the potential of reducing development efforts, facilitating integration of new modules, and minimizing the need for back-end development efforts for new applications (http://www.okiproject.org). An example of a project using O.K.I. Service Interface Definitions is Coursework at Stanford University (http://coursework.stanford.edu).

Another perspective on technical standards is the approach being taken by the American Society for Training and Development (ASTD) and their E-Learning Courseware Certification (ECC). This program is designed to evaluate the instructional design and usability factors of asynchronous Web-based and multimedia courseware. Such courseware must meet rigorous standards based on criteria established by their Certification Standards Committee. These standards include Interface Standards that address the relationship between the learner and the courseware itself; Compatibility Standards that address the relationship between the courseware, the operating system, and related applications; Production Quality Standards that examine the quality of the courseware's text, graphics, grammar, and visual presentation; and Instructional Design Standards that examine the relationship between the course purpose, objectives, instructional content, instructional methods, and the learner. Using such certification, ASTD believes that, with training, consumers could select courseware that demonstrates the characteristics of good instruction (http://www.astd.org/astd/Marketplace/ecc/ecc_home.htm).

4.3 Utilize Outcome Measures

An overarching perspective of measuring outcomes is to use the standard formative and summative evaluation approaches that are integral components of the instructional design processes (Smith & Ragan, 1999, pp. 337-369). There should be a concern with learning outcomes, learner satisfaction, and learner experiences (e.g., type of interactions), but attention should also be placed on gathering data on instructor satisfaction. It is also important to consider the use of multiple measures, such as use of expert reviews, field trials, quantitative and qualitative research designs, performance assessment, and attitudinal assessment.

From a management perspective, outcome measures can include enrollments, costs and cost savings, case studies of the innovative uses of technology, the effectiveness of distance learning as compared to other training methods, and the evaluation of the technical implementation process.

Bersin (2003) discusses e-learning analytics or the data that are used to measure efficiency (revenue, costs), effectiveness (enrollments, completion, scores, certification numbers, improvements), and compliance (certification rates and percentages). He also notes that different data are used by different users to assist in decision making. For example: Executives require overall metrics, financials, compliance efficiency; line managers need data on compliance and skill development; and training personnel require data on training volumes, completion rates, vendor effectiveness. It should be noted that data for e-learning analytics can be generated as a component of some LMS, such as Saba, which has aggregation, grouping, filtering, drilling down, drilling up, charting and subtotaling features; the ability to build custom reports and analyses; and the ability to extract data into other analytic data systems (http://www.saba.com/english/about/analytics/index.htm).

A report on the quality and effectiveness of e-learning (SRI, 2003) identifies a series of variables that can impact the quality of an e-learning program. These variables include interoperability of content and the LMS, continued funding for the program, use of outside contractors, coordination with human resources, support from the information technology department, quality/speed of user computers, and availability of bandwidth. The same report provides a list of methods useful to gauge the effectiveness of distance learning, including cost savings, customer satisfaction, bottom-line gains, manager/mentor reporting, learner self-reporting, learner assessment/testing, numbers of learners trained, and return-on-investment (ROI) analysis. A result of analysis of outcomes should lead to recommendations for improvement. The SRI report identifies the following as common recommendations:

more engaging off-the-shelf content, more customized content, better learning management capabilities, greater personalization of e-learning, greater use of synchronous tools, improved integration/interoperability, and more high-level support for e-learning.

5. References:

Benjamin Franklin Institute of Global Education. (2003). *Distance education—Quality Assurance Institute.* Retrieved September 2, 2003, from http//www.academyweb.com/deqa.htm

Bersin, J. (2003). E-Learning analytics. *Learning Circuits.* American Society for Training and Development. Retrieved July 20, 2002, from http://www.learningcircuits.org/2003/jun2003/bersin.htm

Phipps, R., & Merisotis, J., (2000). *Quality on the line: Benchmarks for success in Internet-based distance education.* Washington DC: The Institute for Higher Education Policy.

Quality Assurance Agency for Higher Education. (n.d.). *Distance learning guidelines.* Retrieved May 10, 2007, from www.qaa.ac.uk/academicinfrastructure/codeofpractice/distancelear ning/default.asp

Smith, P. L., & Ragan, T. J. (Eds.). (1999). *Instructional design* (2nd ed.). Upper Saddle River, NJ: Merrill.

SRI Consulting Business Intelligence. (2003). *Quality and effectiveness of e-learning: A survey of e-learning practitioners.* SRI Consulting Business Intelligence. American Society for Training and Development. Retrieved July 6, 2003, from http://www.sric-bi.com/LoD/summaries/QEelearning2003-04.shtml

Western Interstate Commission for Higher Education. (1997). *Educational telecommunications. Good practices in distance education* (Pub. #2A299). Retrieved May 10, 2007, from http://www.wiche.edu/pubs/cart_subj.asp?pub_id=135

6. Glossary:

Formative evaluation: Formative evaluation typically involves gathering information during the early stages of a project or program, with a focus on finding out whether efforts are unfolding as planned, uncovering any obstacles, barriers or unexpected opportunities that may have emerged, and identifying mid-course adjustments and corrections which can help insure the success of the work. *Northwest Regional Education Laboratory.* Retrieved

August 9, 2003, from
http://www.nwrel.org/evaluation/formative.shtml

Interoperability: The ability of hardware or software components to work together effectively. American Society for Training and Development. *Learning Circuits.* E-Learning Glossary. Retrieved August 9, 2003, from
http://www.learningcircuits.org/glossary.html

Open specifications/architecture: An architecture whose specifications are public. This includes officially approved standards as well as privately designed architectures whose specifications are made public by the designers. The opposite of open is closed or proprietary. The great advantage of open architectures is that anyone can design add-on products for them. By making an architecture public, however, a manufacturer allows others to duplicate its product. *Webopedia.* Retrieved August 9, 2003, from
http://www.webopedia.com/TERM/O/open_architecture.html

Summative evaluation: Summative evaluation typically involves the preparation of a formal report outlining the impact of a program. For instance, an evaluation report will typically detail who participated in a program, what activities affected them, and what gains or improvements resulted from their participation. Often this report will include details regarding what prerequisites or conditions are essential or helpful to the replication of the program, program costs and benefits, and disaggregated results showing findings for specific subgroups of participants. Much of the information gathered during formative evaluation activities may also be reported in formal summative reports. *Northwest Regional Education Laboratory.* Retrieved August 9, 2003, from
http://www.nwrel.org/evaluation/summative.shtml

XML (Extensible Markup Language): The next-generation Webpage coding language that allows site designers to program their own markup commands, which can then be used as if they were standard HTML commands. E-Learning Glossary. *Learning Circuits.* American Society for Training and Development. Retrieved August 9, 2003, from
http://www.learningcircuits.org/glossary.html

7. Checklist:

Strategies Based on Quality Assurance (check yes/no)	Yes	No
Develop General Measures		
Are there benchmark measures on:		
1. Organizational support in terms of a documented, integrative technology plan?		
2. Organizational support in terms of organizational commitment to distance learning?		
3. Organizational support in terms of an adequate budget?		
4. Organizational support in terms of an established program, design, approval, and review process?		
5. Organizational support in terms of a reliable technology delivery system?		
6. Organizational support in terms of adequate infrastructure?		
7. Course development in terms of minimum standards for design, development, delivery?		
8. Course development in terms of instructional materials review?		
9. Course development in terms of student engagement?		
10. Teaching/learning in terms of appropriate academic rigor?		
11. Teaching/learning in terms of the use of qualified instructional personnel?		
12. Teaching/learning in terms of student/student and student/instructor interaction?		
13. Teaching/learning in terms of adequate feedback?		
14. Course structure in terms of student advisement regarding the distance learning program and requirements?		
15. Course structure in terms of course information and requirements?		
16. Course structure in terms of library and virtual information resources?		
17. Course structure in terms of assignment expectation agreement between faculty/student?		
18. Student support in terms of advisement, admissions, requirements, tuition, books, technical requirements?		
19. Student support in terms of student training and informational materials?		
20. Student support in terms of technical assistance?		
21. Student support in terms of adequate question response system and structured complaint resolution system?		
22. Faculty support in terms of adequate compensation?		
23. Faculty support in terms of transitioning from classroom to online teaching?		

	Yes	No
24. Faculty support in terms of training?		
25. Faculty support in terms of technical assistance?		
26. Faculty support in terms of resources to assist in resolving ethical issues associated with use of e-materials?		
27. Evaluation and assessment in terms of use of several methods?		
28. Evaluation and assessment in terms of application of specific standards?		
29. Evaluation and assessment in terms of use of data to evaluate program effectiveness?		
30. Evaluation and assessment in terms of regular review of desired learning outcomes?		
Employ Standards Adherence		
Is there adherence to established standards?		
31. ISO 9000?		
32. AICC?		
33. IMS?		
34. SCORM?		
35. O.K.I.?		
36. ASTD's ECC?		
Utilize Outcome Measures		
37. Are standard formative evaluation methods employed?		
38. Are standard summative evaluation methods employed?		
39. Are measures available on learner outcomes?		
40. Are measures available on performance?		
41. Are measures available on learner experiences?		
42. Are measures available on learner satisfaction?		
43. Are measures available on learner attitudes?		
44. Are measures available on instructor satisfaction?		
45. Are measures available on instructor attitudes?		
46. Are there data on enrollments?		
47. Are there data on scores?		
48. Are there data on completion?		
49. Are there data on certification?		
50. Are there data on compliance?		
51. Are there data on design, development, implementation costs?		
52. Are there data on cost savings?		
53. Are there data on return on investment (ROI)?		
54. Are there data on bottom-line gains?		
55. Are there case studies available of distance learning efforts?		

136

	Yes	No
56. Are there data on the effectiveness of distance learning as compared to other approaches?		
57. Are there data on the technical implementation process?		
58. Are there data on vendor/contractor performance?		
59. Are there data on technical integration (interoperability) of systems?		
60. Are there data on customer satisfaction?		
61. Is there an evaluation report that addresses the overall cost-effectiveness of distance learning?		

Strategies Based on Library and Information Systems and Services

1. Guideline: For a distance learning program to succeed there must be appropriate library and information systems and services.

2. Task Scenario: Build a library and information system that supports a distance learning program by providing options for information services, and plan for the integration of the system and services as components of the learning space.

3. Personnel: External

4. Options: 4.1 Use Physical Collections(s) and Local Library Resources
In some instances, particularly where a traditional course/program is converted to distance, an already existing print collection of books, journals, and reports may be available. However, such a collection becomes less accessible as the distance of learners increases from the collection site. One solution that has been utilized to improve access to print resources is the development of reciprocal use and/borrowing agreements that allow access to library resources and collections at various local sites, such as at local college and public libraries. Another approach to improve access has been to develop agreements whereby physical library reserves can be housed at public libraries at various locations.

4.2 Use Distributed Print Resources
If there is heavy reliance on internally generated or publicly available reports/documents, these materials could be mailed to the students. But this creates a level of personnel and mailing costs that must be factored into the course/program cost. Many courses/programs have associated readers or coursepacks of materials, such as journal articles and chapters of books. An integral component of creating such a system is a copyright clearing process for these materials. To facilitate compliance, various organizations, such as the Copyright Clearance Center, Inc., provide a process whereby permissions can be acquired for copyrighted materials for coursepacks and readers, as well as for Web sites, and e-reserves (http://www.copyright.com).

4.3 Use Internet Resources (Nonbook and Journal Materials)
The Web has an enormous amount of digital resources that can be used in conjunction with a distance learning course/program. Most of these materials have been developed especially for the Web and do not have print counterparts. A search using one of the standard search engines will generate a wealth of materials that may have course relevance. For example, an examination of Internet

resources would lead to a number of sites appropriate to the interest in distance learning, especially relating to learning and instructional strategies. One resource is *Explorations in Learning & Instruction: The Theory Into Practice (TIP) Database.* TIP is a tool intended to make learning and instructional theory more accessible by maintaining a database of brief summaries with additional Web reference links for 50 major theories of learning and instruction. These theories can also be accessed by learning domains and concepts (http://www.gwu.edu/~tip/index.html).

4.4 Use Electronic Reference, Online Journals, and Database Services
There is a rich package of online catalogs and reference services available on the Web, including those that are publicly available and those with restricted use. Some of these are now including full text access to resources. Examples of publicly accessible online catalogs include most library catalogs, such as that at the University of Southern California (http://www.usc.edu/e_resources/isd/). Such online library catalogs can be especially useful to distance students, who then have the ability to locate local library resources.

There are many publicly available reference services, such as the Department of Energy (DOE) Technical Standards that provide access to a great range of handbooks aimed to provide DOE benchmarks for standards (http://www.standards.doe.gov). Another example, connected to the topic of distance learning, is Learning Circuits Online Glossary of E-Learning (http://www.learningcircuits.org/glossary.html).

There are also publicly accessible online journals. For example, again connecting to the interest in distance learning, the *Online Journal of Distance Learning Administration* is a peer-reviewed electronic journal offered free each quarter over the World Wide Web. The *Journal* includes articles on the original work of practitioners and researchers with a specific focus on implications for the management of distance education programs (http://www.westga.edu/~distance/jmain11.html).

Some resources have varying degrees of accessibility. For example, IEEE *Xplore* provides full-text access to IEEE transactions, journals, magazines, and conference proceedings published since 1988 and all current IEEE Standards. All users have free browse and access capability to tables of contents of IEEE transactions, journals, magazines, conference proceedings, and standards. IEEE members have the same capability but are also able to browse or search to access any IEEE abstract/citation record as well as articles from IEEE *Spectrum Magazine* (http://ieeexplore.ieee.org/Xplore/DynWel.jsp).

There are resources that have restricted use and an organization needs to subscribe or establish a system for pay-for-view in order to access online full-text catalogs, databases, and journals. One example is LexisNexis, which through their Academic Service provides full-text documents from over 5,600 news, business, legal, medical, and reference publications with a variety of flexible search options (http://www.lexisnexis.com/).

There are commercial products that help organize these information resource-intensive Web resources, one example being SerialsSolutions, which streamlines e-journal management through providing access by including them in the OPAC (Online Pubic Access Catalog), and can, for example, generate a comprehensive list of electronic journal titles from all the organization's electronic resources that contain full text (http://serialssolutions.com/Home.asp).

4.5 Use Document Delivery Services
Increasingly, journal publishers are making the content of their journals available online. However, this content tends to only cover recent issues and, of course, all resources are not available in e-format nor can each library subscribe to all resources. A system needs to be in place that will send students hardcopy materials or photocopies of desired resources that are located elsewhere. Traditionally, this is part of the library, interlibrary loan services, where physical materials can be borrowed from another library, or resources copied from libraries elsewhere. To support such a service, systems are in place to facilitate such resource sharing, such as use of the Ariel software for document delivery. For example, with commercially available hardware and Ariel software, articles, photos, and other documents can be scanned directly and transmitted electronically to other Ariel workstations anywhere in the world, using either FTP or e-mail. Ariel also allows their conversion to PDF for easy patron delivery. Ariel stands up to difficult text, from Asian scripts to mathematical equations, and handles detailed images (http://www4.infotrieve.com/ariel/).

4.6 Use Course Electronic Reserves
Journal articles, book chapters, exams, and many other materials can be digitized and made accessible via an e-reserve system, such as the reserve system available through Docutek

(http://www.docutek.com/), or as a component of an Online Public Access Catalog (OPAC), for example, SIRSI (http://www.sirsi.com). An integral component of such a system is a copyright clearing process for copyrighted materials.

4.7 Use Reference Consultation and Instructor Support

Library staff can guide users through assisting in database search strategies, provide actual searching of databases, find resources in reference sources, and provide locations of materials available via interlibrary loan. Such a service can provide consultation, answers to reference questions, and identification of resources. Reference librarians can be available via telephone or chat service during normal service hours, or via email reference.

4.8 Use Online Research and User Guides

Library staff members can develop an in-depth resource of research sources and services, a virtual reference system, Websites, and other related materials that can become a part of a course syllabus. For example, Sloan and Stoerger (2002) have developed a guide on library resources for the support of distance learning (http://alexia.lis.uiuc.edu/~b-sloan/libdist.htm).

4.9 Integrate the Various Options

The use of library system software available from vendors, such as that available from Innovative Library Services, can add to the success of the distance learning program. For example, their integrated Millennium system supports the automation of traditional library functions such as cataloging, online public access catalog, circulation, acquisitions, serials control, interlibrary loan, materials booking, and inventory control, as well as advanced capabilities such as real-time resource sharing (union catalog), universal searching, imaging, e-books, content linking, advanced search capabilities, and other Web-based applications. Millennium also includes a suite of digital collections products: electronic resource management for digital resource integration and license management; metadata description capability for digital object cataloging, display and storage; metadata searching, linking, and authentication; and an XML Server, to output catalog data in XML format (http://www.iii.com/).

Contracting with an existing library system is a viable option. For example, eArmyU uses GALILEO (Georgia Library Learning Online), a World Wide Web-based virtual library. GALILEO provides access to multiple information resources, including secured access to licensed products. Participating institutions may access databases indexing thousands of periodicals and scholarly journals. Thousands of journal titles are provided in full-text. Other resources include online encyclopedias, business directories, and government publications (http://www.usg.edu/galileo/).

Ease of access to library resources and services is essential, and this access should be interoperable with the CMS or LMS.

5. References: Sloan, B., & Stoerger, S. (2002). *Library support for distance learning*. Retrieved July 8, 2003, from http://alexia.lis.uiuc.edu/~b-sloan/libdist.htm

6. Glossary: **Course management system (CMS):** A course management system, or CMS, is usually software that has capabilities in three areas: (a) design interface and content assembly; (b) the facilitation of communication and collaboration; and (c) course management support used to manage the content of a Web site. *Educause Effective Practices and Solutions*. Retrieved August 16, 2007, from http://www.educause.edu/ir/library/pdf/DEC0302.pdf

Interlibrary loan: This is the process by which a library requests material from, or supplies material to, another library. The purpose of interlibrary loan, as defined by the Interlibrary Loan Code for the United States, is to obtain, upon request of a library user, material not available in the user's local library. *American Library Association, Interlibrary loan code for the United States (2001)*. Retrieved August 16, 2007, from http://www.ala.org/ala/rusa/rusaprotools/referenceguide/interlibrary.htm

Learning management system (LMS): Software that automates the administration of training. The LMS registers users, tracks courses, records data from learners, and provides reports to management. An LMS is typically designed to handle courses by multiple publishers and providers. It usually doesn't include its own authoring capabilities; instead, it focuses on managing courses created by a variety of other sources. E-Learning Glossary. *Learning Circuits*. American Society for Training and Development. Retrieved August 8, 2003, from http://www.learningcircuits.org/glossary.html

Metadata: Information about content that allows it to be stored and retrieved from a database or web-site. E-Learning Glossary. *Learning Circuits*. American Society for Training and Development. Retrieved July 20, 2002, from http://www.learningcircuits.org/glossary.html

OPAC (Online Public Access Catalog): An online bibliography of a library collection that is available to the public. Most libraries have made their OPAC accessible from a server to users all over the world. User searches of an OPAC make use of the Z39.50 protocol that can also be used to link disparate OPACS into a single "union" OPAC. *searchDatabase.com Definitions.* Retrieved August 22, 2003, from http://searchdatabase.techtarget.com/sDefinition/0,,sid13_gci213451,00.html

XML (Extensible Markup Language): The next-generation Webpage coding language that allows site designers to program their own markup commands, which can then be used as if they were standard HTML commands. E-Learning Glossary. *Learning Circuits.* American Society for Training and Development. Retrieved August 9, 2003, from http://www.learningcircuits.org/glossary.html

7. Checklist:

Strategies Based on Library and Information Systems and Services (check yes/no)	Yes	No
Use Physical Collections(s) and Local Library Resources		
1. Is there an existing print collection of books, journals, and reports available?		
2. Is there a reciprocal library use and borrowing agreement at local library sites?		
3. Can library materials be house at local public or other libraries?		
Use Distributed Print Resources		
4. Can readers or coursepacks be generated?		
5. Is there a procedure for obtaining copyright clearance for materials?		
6. Can library materials/resources and readers/coursepacks be mailed to students?		
Use Internet Resources (Nonbook AND Journal Materials)		
7. Are there appropriate Internet resources available?		

	Yes	No
Use Electronic Reference, Online Journals, and Database Services		
8. Are there publicly available, relevant Web library catalogs and reference services that provide access to local site materials?		
9. Are there publicly available, relevant Web library catalogs and reference services that provide full-text access to books, journals, documents, and other resources?		
10. Are there subscription services available that provide access to appropriate Web resources?		
Use Document Delivery Services		
11. Is there a system in place to request materials located at other libraries?		
12. Is there a hardcopy (books or photocopy) document delivery service?		
13. Is there a fax document delivery service?		
14. Is there an email/PDF format document delivery service?		
Use Course Electronic Reserves		
15. Are there materials that can be digitized and made accessible via an e-reserve system?		
16. Is there a procedure for obtaining copyright clearance for e-reserve materials?		
Use Reference Consultation and Instructor Support		
17. Is there library reference service via telephone?		
18. Is there library reference service via email?		
19. Is there synchronous library reference service?		
20. Are there interlibrary loan services?		
Use Online Research and User Guides		
21. Are there in-depth resources and/or user guides of research sources and services available?		
Integrate Various Options		
22. Is there library system software available to support the myriad of library information systems and services?		
23. Is there the use of an existing Web-based library system for systems and services?		
24. Are library systems and services integrated with the existing CMS/LMS?		

Strategies Based on Content Management

1. Guideline:

Develop opportunities to exchange and reuse the content of distance learning.

2. Task Scenario:

Monitor and be proactive regarding the developments in content management and in the reuse and interoperation among learning systems.

3. Personnel:

External

4. Options:

4.1 Monitor Development in Learning Content Management Systems

Considerable content is produced for learning applications, and there is the desire to be able to reuse and repurpose this content. Rather than develop new learning-specific content, an option is to access content libraries to assist in gathering content for course development, to be used either as a component of a course or as a stand-alone entity. The overall impact of such an approach is to accelerate product deployment, as well as potentially reduce costs and add value. A learning content management system (LCMS) facilitates the creation, rapid deployment, and management of content objects. Examples of LCMS include products from Gemini Learning Systems, Inc. (http://www.gemini.com/home.html) and Click2Learn, Inc. (http://www.asymetrix.com/). Typically, an LCMS provides an authoring tool and a user interface, supports administrative functions, and contains a repository for learning objects. Content objects, or learning objects, are decontextualized from the medium or presentation format, and consist of reusable digital resources, including such items as tutorials, audio and video clips, simulations, images, Websites, and assessments, as well as more traditionally viewed libraries and information resources. Reusable learning objects (RLO) are the smallest independent instructional experience that contains an objective, a learning activity, and an assessment (Nichani, 2001). Storage and retrieval of learning objects requires educational metadata, or more specifically, learning objects metadata (LOM), which are a minimal set of attributes that provide a means for users to locate learning resources applicable to their own contexts. As a point of comparison, in contrast to a LCMS, which is primarily concerned with managing the content of learning objects, a learning management system (LMS) is primarily focused on managing learners and their performance progress; and a course management system (CMS) is primarily concerned with managing course content and learner profiles. Both can provide approaches for developers to recontextualize the learning objects. It should be

145

noted that there is the need for interoperability of CMS, LMS, and LCMS. Some LCMS also have built-in LMS functionality (Brandon-Hall Research (n.d). *LMS & LCMS demystified*).

There are various characteristics required for adequate storage and retrieval of learning objects, such as a database repository and version control of the content. Longmire (2000) noted that the use of learning objects impacts the work of instructional designers and identified several requirements. These include, for example, the need for consistency in assigning descriptive terminology about the content; developing presentations in accessible and comprehensive formats (e.g., charts/graphs rather than dense text); developing presentations of information for onscreen use; designing for nonsequentiality (e.g., not referencing prior or future content); and using language geared towards broad audiences.

Reusable learning content can be generated internally within an organization or can be procured from a learning partner, for example, NETg (http://www.netg.com). In addition, there is a useful development that assists users in locating learning content. MERLOT (Multimedia Educational Resource for Learning and Online Teaching) is a free collection of online learning materials supported by a collaborative effort of higher education institutions. MERLOT provides a description of the content that is stored elsewhere on the Internet. Included for each of the learning materials are such elements as type of content, subject categories, description, the author, the URL, peer review comments, a thumbnail image of learning material, target audience, cost, and licensing and copyright information (http://www.merlot.org/).

An issue that needs to be addressed relates to the incorporation of learning objects into the instructional design process. Wiley (2001) discussed many relevant topics on the issue, such as the possible use of learning objects in a constructivist learning environment, and the application of learning objects in the design of resource-based learning, performance support systems, and inquiry-based learning.

5. References:

Brandon-Hall Research. (n.d). *LMS & LCMS demystified* Retrieved August 17, 2007, from http://www.brandon-hall.com/free_resources/lms_and_lcms.shtml

Longmire, W. (2000). *A primer on learning objects*. American Society for Training and Development. Retrieved August 16, 2007, from http://www.learningcircuits.org/2000/mar2000/Longmire.htm

Nichani, M. (2001). LCMS=LMS + CMS [RLOs]. *elearningpost.* Retrieved July 5, 2003, from http://www.elearningpost.com/features/archives/001022.asp

Wiley, D. A. (2001). Connecting learning objects to instructional design theory: A definition, a metaphor, and a taxonomy. In D. A. Wiley (Ed.), *The instructional use of learning objects.* Association for Instructional Technology and the Association for Educational Communications and Technology. American Society for Training and Development. Retrieved July 7, 2003, from http://www.reusability.org/read/

6. Glossary:

Course management system (CMS): A course management system (CMS) is usually software that has capabilities in three areas: (1) design interface and content assembly; (2) the facilitation of communication and collaboration; and (3) course management support. *Course management systems (CMS).* Retrieved August 17, 2007, from http://www.educause.edu/ir/library/pdf/DEC0302.pdf

Interoperation/Interoperability: The ability of hardware or software components to work together effectively. E-Learning Glossary. *Learning Circuits.* American Society for Training and Development. Retrieved July 20, 2002, from http://www.learningcircuits.org/glossary.html

Learning content management system (LCMS): A software application that allows trainers and training directors to manage both the administrative and content-related functions of training. An LCMS combines the course management capabilities of an LMS (learning management system) with the content creation and storage capabilities of a CMS (content management system). Includes learning objects, the reusable, media independent chunks of information used as modular building blocks for e-learning content. E-Learning Glossary. *Learning Circuits.* American Society for Training and Development. Retrieved July 20, 2002, from http://www.learningcircuits.org/glossary.html

Learning management system (LMS): Software that automates the administration of training. The LMS registers users, tracks courses, records data from learners, and provides reports to management. An LMS is typically designed to handle courses by multiple publishers and providers. It usually doesn't include its own authoring capabilities; instead, it focuses on managing courses created by a variety of other sources. E-Learning Glossary. *Learning Circuits.* American Society for Training and

Development. Retrieved August 8, 2003, from
http://www.learningcircuits.org/glossary.html

Learning objects metadata (LOM): LOM is defined as the
attributes, or metadata (see definition), required to fully/adequately
describe a Learning Object. Learning Objects are defined here as
any entity, digital or non-digital, which can be used, re-used or
referenced during technology supported learning. *IEEE Draft
standard for learning object metadata IEEE 1484.12.1-2002.*
Retrieved August 17, 2007, from http://ltsc.ieee.org/wg12/files
/LOM_1484_12_1_v1_Final_Draft.pdf

Metadata: Information about content that allows it to be stored
and retrieved from a database or web-site; learning objects are
most effective when organized by a metadata classification system
and stored in a data repository such as a LCMS. E-Learning
Glossary. *Learning Circuits.* American Society for Training and
Development. Retrieved July 20, 2002, from
http://www.learningcircuits.org/glossary.html

Reusable learning object (RLO): A collection of reusable
information objects (a group of content, practice, and assessment
items assembled around a single learning objective), or overview,
summary, and assessments that support a specific learning
objective. E-Learning Glossary. *Learning Circuits.* American
Society for Training and Development. Retrieved August 8, 2003,
from http://www.learningcircuits.org/glossary.html

7. Checklist:

Strategy Elements for Content Management (check yes/no)	Yes	No
Monitor Development in Learning Content Management Systems (LCMS)		
1. Does the learning system (LMS or CMS) provide for the management of the learning content (LCMS)?		
2. Does the LCMS have interoperability with an LMS/CMS?		
3. Is there the ability to create learning objects?		
4. Is there the ability to store learning objects?		
5. Is there adequate metadata for learning objects?		
6. Is there ability for users to input descriptions of content?		
7. Is there version control of the content?		

	Yes	No
8. Is there the ability of users to add comments or annotations about the content?		
9. Is there the ability to access and retrieve learning objects internally across the organization?		
10. Is there the ability to access and retrieve learning objects externally from outside the organization?		
11. Is there a powerful search engine for retrieval of objects in the repository?		
12. Can content be redeployed in a variety of formats?		
13. Are there strategies in place to facilitate the incorporation of learning objects into instructional design?		

Strategies Based on Student Support Services

1. Guideline: Distance learning participants need support for success.

2. Task Scenario: Provide an appropriate learner support environment with assistance in counseling, scheduling and registration, problem solving, mentoring, delivery of course materials, and maintenance of appropriate records and transcripts.

3. Personnel: External

4. Options: 4.1 Develop Pre-Admissions Support

Student support services are central to the success of a distance learning program, and these services need to be of the same standard as those available in nondistance modes. Various distance learning guidelines call attention to the need for appropriate student services (Bunn, 2001; Cho & Berge, 2002; Gellman-Danley & Fetzner, 1998). The literature, for example, on virtual advising (Wagner, 2001) identifies best practices, such as clear and concise explanation of curriculum, advisement FAQs, information for all students and for special population groups, and one-to-one access to advisors via chat rooms, listservs, and emails. There are a myriad of student services that need attention; the first of these relate to pre-admission. Information should be available via the Website on the program, courses, faculty/instructors, requirements, admission procedures, and appropriate contact procedures for further information.

4.2. Implement Enrollment and Advisement Subsystems

There are numerous components to successful enrollment and advisement for distance learning. Procedures should be in place for online admissions materials submission, online class schedules, and an online and/or phone system registration. Students need accurate and supporting information regarding enrollment costs, including tuition and fees; payment options and procedures for refunds; withdrawals; discounts; financial aid and loans; tuition assistance; and veterans' benefits. Another service, pre-enrollment skill assessment and placement testing, can be beneficial to student success. Also a procedure must be in place for generating and distributing student identification cards, including a library card, if necessary.

4.3 Provide Ongoing Course and Program Support

Ongoing support is a major factor for positive student attitudes towards distance learning and to students' learning success, with technical support being a contributing success factor. Initially, technical support includes providing any computer software, software license agreements, and installation assistance. As appropriate, this might include an entire technology package of required and supported hardware and software. Initial technology support also typically entails assistance in setting up accounts, for example, e-mail, and necessary network connections. On an ongoing basis, there is the need for technical support and information, such as through an on-call computer helpdesk, e-mail service, online documentation, and FAQs. Instructional resource support is provided through a system that distributes textbooks and other course materials, such as the eArmyU use of MBS Direct (http://www.mbsbooks.com/direct/) for course material distribution. It is essential to have library and information resource access and, if applicable, the issuance of a library card to be used at remote locations (e.g., public libraries) that might offer supporting library services for the distance learning program. And, as needed, services and facilities might be required for administering and proctoring examinations.

4.4 Develop Record-Keeping and Maintenance Subsystems
Considerable amounts of data are generated regarding student performance in distance learning efforts, and these data must be maintained over time. Such data and records include course credits and grades with the need to be able to generate transcripts on demand. In addition, data on certificate and program requirement compliance and degree progress must be maintained and used for certificate and degree audits, and for graduation purposes. Procedures must be in place for articulation and course transfer agreements with other institutions and organizations.

4.5 Implement Overall Support
In addition to enrollment and advisement, ongoing support, and record-keeping services, various other support services are options, and yet can assist in making the distance learning experience of students successful. These might include, for example, diagnostic services and FAQs to assist in determining the readiness of students for distance learning, and short online courses on strategies for success (e.g., learning to learn). Other academic support services could include person-to-person online tutoring, an online writing lab, independent study resources, English as a Second Language (ESL) courses, and other academic assistance. For example, real-time academic support is provided to students in eArmyU through Smarthinking (http://www.SMARTHINKING.com). At the end of the spectrum of support, career development services might be offered to develop, evaluate, and assist students in implementing career

plans. Additional support concerns include facilitating the development of online small learner communities for sharing and support; and providing health services and services for students with disabilities and special needs.

4.6 Consider Other Factors
There are various elements that need to be in place to support overall student services. From the policy and procedures perspective this includes having operationalized student service policies and rules of student conduct—for example, regarding copyright infringement and appropriate computer use. Another policy issue is concerned with the extent of use of service partners for student services in logistical support, program mentoring, and administrative activities. From the technical perspective there must be concern about the scalability of service support; the interface for authentification purposes with student information systems (e.g., registration), and with the CMS or LMS; and the ability to access easily student services information through the learning system.

5. References:

Bunn, M. D. (2001). Timeless and timely issues in distance education planning. *The American Journal of Distance Education, 13*(1), 55-67.

Cho, S. K., & Berge, Z. L. (2002). Overcoming barriers to distance training and education. *United States Distance Learning Association Journal, 16*(1). Retrieved July 11, 2002, from http://www.usdla.org/html/journal/JAN02_Issue/article01.html

Gellman-Danley, B., & Fetzner, M. J. (1998). Asking the really tough questions: Policy issues for distance education. *Online Journal of Distance Learning Administration, 1*(1). Retrieved August 17, 2007, from http://www.westga.edu/~distance/ojdla/spring11/danley11.pdf

Wagner, L. (2001). Virtual advising: Delivering student services. *Online Journal of Distance Learning Administration, 4*(3). Retrieved July 20, 2002, from http://www.westga.edu/~distance/ojdla/fall43/wagner43.html

6. Glossary:

FAQ (Frequently Asked Questions): An informational list, in question-and-answer format, of common inquiries from users about a topic or application and standard responses. FAQs appear on Websites and discussion boards and within desktop applications. E-Learning Glossary. *Learning Circuits.* American

Society for Training and Development. Retrieved August 8, 2003, from http://www.learningcircuits.org/glossary.html

7. *Checklist:*

Strategies Based on Student Support Services (check yes/no)	Yes	No
Develop Pre-Admissions Support		
1. Is there information available via the Web on the program?		
2. Is there information available via the Web on the courses?		
3. Is there information available via the Web on faculty and instructors?		
4. Is there information available via the Web on program requirements?		
5. Is there information available via the Web on appropriate contacts and application procedures?		
Implement Enrollment and Advisement Subsystems		
6. Is there a system in place for online admissions materials submission?		
7. Is there information available via the Web on class schedules?		
8. Is there a system in place for online and/or phone registration?		
9. Is there readily available information on tuition and fees?		
10. Is there readily available information on payment options?		
11. Is there readily available information on procedures for refunds?		
12. Is there readily available information on withdrawals?		
13. Is there readily available information on discounts?		
14. Is there readily available information on financial aid and loans?		
15. Is there readily available information on tuition assistance?		
16. Is there readily available information on veterans' benefits?		
17. Is there a system in place for online payment of any tuition and fees?		
18. Is there a system in place for generating and distributing identification card(s)?		
Provide Ongoing Course and Program Support		
19. Is there initial technical support regarding computer software, computer software licenses, and software installation?		
20. Is there initial support regarding procurement and installation of technology packages of required hardware and software?		
21. Is there initial technical support regarding setting up accounts, e.g., an email account?		
22. Is there initial technical support regarding network connections?		
23. Is there a computer on-call helpdesk?		
24. Is there an email helpdesk function?		

	Yes	No
25. Is there online documentation ?		
26. Are there online FAQs?		
27. Is there a textbook and other resource ordering and distribution system?		
28. Is there an online library and information resource system?		
29. Are library identification cards provided?		
30. Are there services for remote exam taking and proctoring?		
Develop Record-Keeping and Maintenance Subsystems		
31. Is there a system in place to record course credits and grades?		
32. Is there a system in place whereby students can view their grades?		
33. Does the LMS/CMS transmit course grades to the organization's record-keeping and maintenance system?		
34. Is there a system in place to provide transcripts of courses and grades?		
35. Is there a system in place to monitor degree/certification progress?		
36. Is there a system in place to document graduation?		
37. Are there articulation agreements in place?		
Implement Overall Support		
38. Are there diagnostic services in place to determine student readiness?		
39. Are there FAQs relating to student readiness for distance learning?		
40. Are there short courses available for developing strategies for successful distance learning?		
41. Is there online one-to-one tutoring?		
42. Is there an online mentoring service?		
43. Is there an online academic program advisement and support service?		
44. Is there an online writing lab?		
45. Are there online ESL courses?		
46. Is there an online career development service?		
47. Is there information about access to student health services?		
48. Is there information about access to services for students with special needs?		
49. Is there a mechanism to establish online small student learner communities?		

	Yes	No
Consider Other Factors		
50. Are there established student policy guidelines?		
51. Is there a manual of appropriate student conduct?		
52. Are there organizational policies dealing with use of third-party providers for student support services?		
53. Are student support services scalable?		
54. Does the student information system interface with the CMS or LMS for user authentification purposes?		
55. Is information about student services readily accessible via the learning system?		

REFERENCES

Anderson, L. W., Krathwohl, D. R., Airasian, P. W., Cruikshank, K. A., Mayer, R. E., Pintrich, P. R., Raths, J., & Wittrock, M. C. (2001). *A taxonomy for learning, reaching, and assessing.* New York: Longman.

Baker, E. L., Aguirre-Muñoz, Z., Wang, J., & Niemi, D. (2005). Assessment strategies. In H. F. O'Neil (Ed.), *What works in distance learning: Guidelines* (pp. 65-88). Greenwich, CT: Information Age Publishing.

Baker, E. L., O'Neil H. F., Jr., & Linn, R. L. (1992, September). *What works in alternative assessment?* Sherman Oaks, CA: Advance Design Information, Inc.

Clark, R. E. (2005). Instructional strategies. In H. F. O'Neil (Ed.), *What works in distance learning: Guidelines* (pp. 25-39). Greenwich, CT: Information Age Publishing Inc.

Clark, R. C., & Mayer, R. E. (2003). *E-learning and the science of instruction.* San Francisco: Jossey-Bass.

Davenport, T. H., & Glaser, J. (2002). Just-in-time delivery comes to knowledge management. *Harvard Business Review, 80*(7), 107-111.

Dembo, M. H., & Gubler Junge, L. (2005). Learning strategies. In H. F. O'Neil (Ed.), *What works in distance learning: Guidelines* (pp. 41-63). Greenwich, CT: Information Age Publishing Inc.

Ellis A. (1998). *How to control your anxiety before it controls you.* New York: Kensington.

Hansen, M. T., Nohria, N., & Tierney, T. (1999). What's your strategy for managing knowledge? *Harvard Business Review, 77*(2), 106-116.

Kalyuga, S., Chandler, P., Touvinen, J., & Sweller, J. (2001). When problem solving is superior to worked examples. *Journal of Educational Psychology, 93,* 579-588.

Kazlauskas, E. (2005). Management strategies. In H. F. O'Neil (Ed.), *What works in distance learning: Guidelines* (pp. 123-141). Greenwich, CT: Information Age Publishing Inc.

King, A. (1992). Comparison of self-questioning, summarizing, and note taking review as strategies for learning from lectures. *American Educational Research Journal, 29,* 303-323.

King, A. (1994). Autonomy and question asking: The role of personal control in guided student-generated *questioning. Learning and Individual Differences, 6,* 163-185.

Lan, W. Y. (1996). The effects of self-monitoring on students' course performance, use of learning strategies, attitude, self-judgment ability, and knowledge representation. *Journal of Experimental Education, 64,* 101-115.

Mayer, R. E. (2001). *Multimedia learning*. New York: Cambridge University Press.

Mayer, R. E. (2002). Multimedia learning. In B. H. Ross (Ed.), *The psychology of learning and motivation* (vol. 41; pp. 84-140). San Diego: Academic Press.

Mayer, R. E. (2003). *Learning and instruction*. Upper Saddle River, NJ : Pearson Education, Inc.

Mayer, R. E. (2005). Multimedia strategies. In H. F. O'Neil (Ed.), *What works in distance learning: Guidelines* (pp. 7-23). Greenwich, CT: Information Age Publishing Inc.

Montague, W. E. (Ed.). (1988). *What works: Summary of research findings with implications for Navy instruction and learning*. Pensacola, FL: Office of the Chief of Naval Education and Training.

O'Neil, H. F. (Ed.). (2005). *What works in distance learning: Guidelines*. Greenwich, CT: Information Age Publishing Inc.

O'Neil, H. F., & Chuang, S.-H. (2005). Self-regulation strategies. In H. F. O'Neil (Ed.), *What works in distance learning. Guidelines* (pp. 111-121). Greenwich, CT: Information Age Publishing.

Sweller, J. (1999). Instructional design in technical areas. Camberwell, Australia: ACER Press.

U.S. Department of Education. (1986). *What works. Research about teaching and learning*. Washington, DC: U.S. Government Printing Office.

U.S. Department of Education. (1987). *What works. Research about teaching and learning* (2nd ed., IS 87-110). Washington, DC: U.S. Government Printing Office.

Zimmerman, B. J. (1998). Academic studying and the development of personal skill: A self-regulatory perspective. *Educational Psychologist, 33*, 73-86.

Printed in the United States
105776LV00007B/3/P